CALL CENTER AGENT TURNOVER AND RETENTION

The Best of
Call Center Management Review

Second Edition

Revised and Updated with New Material!

Brad Cleveland and Susan Hash, Editors

Call Center Press™
A Division of ICMI, Inc.

Published by:
Call Center Press
A Division of ICMI, Inc.
P.O. Box 6177
Annapolis, Maryland 21401 USA

Copyright 2004 by ICMI, Inc.

Printed in the United States of America

ISBN 1-932558-04-7

Table of Contents

Foreword

Even as call centers continue to rapidly evolve and gain respect, one challenge remains constant: agent turnover. It has been a hot topic of discussion—and debate—ever since human beings first donned a headset. That's not surprising, considering the fact that call center staff attrition—and the resultant rehiring and retraining efforts necessitated by it—costs companies hundreds of thousands of dollars each year.

Fortunately, many progressive call centers are fighting back—implementing effective and proactive agent retention strategies to help keep valued staff in place, costs down and customer satisfaction high. This book contains a host of insightful articles by consultants, managers and other call center experts who have dedicated a large part of their professional careers to battling employee churn, as well as to developing innovating ways to plan for and manage it.

So dig in to discover proven ways to slow the revolving-door effect, and turn your call center into a place where agents will take great pride in performing at their best for years to come.

Sincerely,
The ICMI Team

Chapter 1: The Cost of Turnover

Lost agents equal lost dollars. The costs of constantly having to recruit, assess, train and develop call center staff can sink companies that suffer high employee attrition. And those are just the obvious, easily measurable costs; then there are the costs of lost opportunities and customers that result when service stumbles—as it often does in centers with high agent churn.

An in-depth look at the true costs of staff attrition—and how one progressive call center was able to stop the "bleeding" by focusing on root causes.

Understanding the Costly Threat of Agent Turnover

By Seymour Burchman and Debra Schmitt

The high cost of employee turnover is a serious issue that is devastating to profits, especially in call center services companies. In all U.S. industries last year, the median turnover rate was 15 percent. Yet in the call center services sector, it was more than twice that rate, according to research by Sibson & Company, a global management consulting firm.

Some call centers routinely experience turnover rates well in excess of 100 percent. It's easy to see why turnover is rated by most call center managers as one of the top three managerial challenges. The large cost, compared to both earning and transaction revenues, justifies this concern.

Sibson recently completed a study that focused on frontline employees—those who directly affect a company's customers because they can have a significant impact on revenue generation and growth potential. Let's take a look at the three key areas examined in the study: staff turnover costs, causes and cures.

Understand the True Cost of Agent Turnover

With the jobless rate at a 30-year low, the tight labor market exacerbates the problem of replacing agents who leave. Recruiting new people in a strong economy is more difficult and takes more time. High employee turnover requires companies to spend resources to replace existing employees rather than hiring for growth. Consequently, many companies are forced to operate under capacity, limiting sales and market share growth in a strong economic environment.

Replacing an agent is expensive because of:

1. Direct costs such as recruiting costs, training costs and paying temporary agency fees and overtime.

2. Opportunity costs, which include lost customers due to poor service and quality, decreased productivity and having to operate under capacity.

3. Indirect costs, such as reduced morale, loss of organizational knowledge,

hampered growth rates and inefficient use of corporate staff time.

By solving the employee turnover problem, companies have a great opportunity to improve profitability and stock prices. Yet many companies approach the issue with methods destined for defeat. Other organizations accept turnover as a cost of doing business, without calculating the actual expense.

Understanding the true cost of employee turnover builds the business case for change. The first step is to identify the employee segments that represent the largest turnover costs. In the Sibson study, the focus was on telemarketing service representatives (TSRs) because of their significant impact on revenue generation and growth potential—a company's top line.

In call centers, there are 2.5 million employees in this category and Sibson estimates that the annual direct cost of turnover in corporate and stand-alone call center services companies is $5.4 billion, or 43 percent of industry earnings. When taken to the level of an individual company, this savings not only has a profound effect on earnings, but also on stock price. Assuming a constant price-to-earnings ratio, a 43 percent reduction in earnings translates into a 43 percent reduction in stock price. These calculations represent only direct replacement costs. They do not take into account the opportunity or indirect costs.

Research the Root Causes

Although some companies recognize the high cost of employee turnover and have taken steps to reduce it, many managers find that their efforts reap little value because they implement traditional solutions without truly understanding the root causes of the problem. Actions such as increasing salaries across the enterprise may not produce the expected results because the reasons for employee departures vary from group to group. Without a robust qualitative and quantitative fact base, managers cannot determine root causes or estimate the expected return on turnover reduction efforts.

A recommended methodology for determining the multifaceted causes of employee turnover and creating cost-effective strategies for solving the problem involves three key steps. Managers can develop a solid fact base by:

CALCULATING RETURN ON INVESTMENT

Step 1: Identify direct replacement and opportunity costs:

A. Direct Replacement Costs: $1.3 million
  • Overtime cost of peers to cover open positions
  • Temporary agency fees to cover for open positions
  • Extra overtime by new employees to move up the learning curve
  • Percent of time spent by first-line supervisors addressing turnover
  • Recruiting costs associated with turnover
  • Training costs associated with turnover
  • Separation processing costs

B. Opportunity Costs: $4.4 million
  • Productivity costs
  • Revenue from lost accounts
  • Cost of operating under capacity

Step 2: Estimate ROI of Reducing Turnover

A. Determine Potential Cost Savings
  (Direct + Opportunity Costs) x (Feasible Turnover Reduction Estimate)
  $5.7 million x 50% = $2.8 million

B. Estimate Turnover Reduction Investments
  Training and Recruiting Costs: $440,000
  Recruiting Fees: $20,000
  Reengineering Costs: $200,000
  Total Investment: $660,000

C. Calculate ROI
  ROI = (Potential Cost Savings) / Turnover Reduction Investments x 100%
  $2.8 million/$660,000 = 424%

Step 3: Estimate Impact on Net Income and Market Capitalization

A. Determine Potential Improvement to Net Income
  (Cost Savings - Investments) x (Effective Tax Rate)
  ($2.8 million - $660,000) x (1-40%) = $1.3 million

B. Determine Potential Gain in Market Capitalization
  (Turnover Reduction Improvement on Net Income) x (Price/Earnings Ratio)
  $1.3 million x 10 = $13 million (47% improvement over initial value of $28 million)

Chapter 1

- Examining turnover and operational data by agent population,
- Conducting agent focus groups and using Web-based employee surveys, and
- Analyzing what is causing agents to start looking elsewhere.

This qualitative and quantitative analysis results in the discovery of specific employee populations with the highest costs of turnover, and the causes of this turnover.

Once employee populations are identified, it is often necessary to segment the population even further to clearly identify the costs and root causes of turnover. For instance, in one call center, the employees were segmented into categories of part-time and full-time and then divided again into shifts. The overall turnover rate was 386 percent and the rate for part-time employees was 714 percent. Also, turnover among night-shift people was higher than for day-shift agents. This analysis highlighted for management the employee population where turnover was the greatest.

The next analysis focused on attrition rates. Within one week, more than 20

SELF-PERPETUATING TURNOVER CYCLE

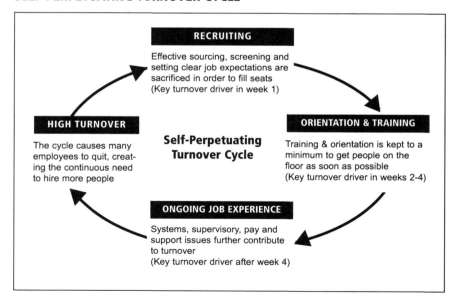

percent of new-hires had resigned. By the end of the first month, more than 40 percent had left. And by the end of six months, the company had lost nearly 75 percent of its new-hires.

The high attrition rate within the first week points to problems in sourcing and recruiting people suited for this type of work. Research revealed that part of the problem was the screening process. During interviews, candidates were not given a clear picture of the job responsibilities, critical skills were not screened for and recruiters were overselling the job. As a result, people who were hired had unrealistic job expectations and inadequate skill sets—setting the stage for high turnover.

The high attrition rate within the first six months—nearly 75 percent—pointed to another problem. Interviews with employees showed dissatisfaction with training and orientation. Initial classroom training was minimal and only covered basic policies and procedures. Moreover, "on-the-job" training was insufficient because of resource constraints and supervisors were ill-prepared to train and coach their employees.

After six months, the research revealed that turnover continued because employees were dissatisfied with their ongoing job experience and the company's employee value proposition. Agents had trouble understanding the pay and time-tracking system, as well as the bonus program. They also complained about inconsistent management practices, especially in the area of attendance. All of these problems, taken together, created a high turnover cycle, which was self-perpetuating.

Base the Cure on the Root Causes

After delineating the root causes of turnover in this group of agents, the next step was to develop creative recommendations that used both traditional and nontraditional measures to solve the root problems. For the call center, analyses showed that investment in several areas would improve the situation.

- The recruiting process was reengineered, including:
  a. Defining the desired knowledge, skills and behaviors of agents and using

this information as the foundation for screening and interviewing candidates.

b. Adding additional recruiters with improved skills.

c. Empowering recruiters to offer higher salaries to more qualified candidates.

d. Scripting interviews so that a realistic picture of the job was provided.

e. Bringing supervisors into the recruiting process. To make it easier for the supervisors to be involved in interviews, a "group interview" was implemented, which provided a social setting in which the candidates could interact with several supervisors and peers.

• A simple database was developed to provide management with up-to-date information on the recruiting, interviewing and hiring decisions. Also, the database tracks the effectiveness of the sourcing mediums and venues (radio, Internet, employee referrals, job fairs, etc.) by calculating the return on the investment.

• With the right talent sitting in the orientation and training sessions, the overall learning curve was reduced by rethinking the approach to training, including:

a. Restructuring the training content to be consistent with the critical agent knowledge, skills and behaviors identified for the recruiting process.

b. Enhancing the overall training experience, moving away from the theoretical to a more practical learning environment by incorporating role-play, simulation and workshops with feedback sessions.

c. Fostering a learning environment, making training readily available; e.g. videos, subject-matter experts, reading material, Web-based training programs, etc.

d. Creating a mentoring and coaching program that identifies development opportunities and a personal training plan for each agent.

• The management and supervisory staff were evaluated based on key competencies for the job. Those who required skill development were given additional training while others were replaced. Promotion and performance appraisal criteria were also adjusted to reflect the newly developed competencies. Further, pay programs were adjusted to reflect the emphasis on people skills.

• The pay programs for agents were revised and new communication programs were introduced to help explain them. Non-cash recognition programs were retooled and expanded.

Measure Results by Savings, Morale and Call Center Image

After implementing the changes, the call center reported significant savings, not only to the bottomline, but to the top line, as well.

The final task, of course, is to ensure the process is ongoing—and to follow up on the agent retention program to measure actual savings and the impact on the company's earnings and stock price. The overall effect of an employee retention program is not only measured in monetary terms, but also in improved agent morale, increased business opportunities and enhanced image of the company in the marketplace.

Chapter 2: Create a Retention-Oriented Culture

Successful agent retention starts with the dominant culture that is promoted within the call center—and the enterprise as a whole. Environments where staff are micro-managed, made to focus on quantity at the expense of quality, and rarely feel empowered are breeding grounds for high turnover. On the other hand, in companies that create a culture of respect and agent-centricity, and that promote careers—not merely jobs—in customer contact, staff will invariably decide to stick around and perform at high levels.

The Role of Corporate Culture in Agent Commitment

by Jean Bave-Kerwin

Creating a career development process won't help you retain agents if your culture is not committed to continual learning.

It's no coincidence that the Digital Products Customer Support call center at Eastman Kodak Co.'s Americas Call Center Operations in Chili, NY, can claim a zero turnover rate for the past two years.

Call center manager Nancy Sweet's approach to creating satisfied customer service agents begins with her understanding of what causes staff burnout, dissatisfaction and internal pressure to leave for a better job.

There's been increasing evidence that a "better" job to employees isn't necessarily a higher-paying one. Instead, workers are looking for satisfaction in the type of work performed, respectful treatment by the company, coaching and feedback, and the opportunity to learn new skills—all of which are aspects of company culture.

Well-known customer loyalty expert Frederick Reichheld commented in *CIO Enterprise Magazine* that the key to an effective corporate culture is to systematically implement programs which improve "specific aspects of the working environment," rather than to mistakenly assume that better benefits equal a better culture. And the "telltale sign of an effective corporate culture is loyalty—the percentage of employees and customers who stay with the company."

Then, apparently, Kodak is doing something right. In fact, the company has a set of values that are explicit, widely held and clearly understood by all employees. They are:

- Respect for individual dignity
- Uncompromising integrity
- Trust
- Credibility
- Continuous improvement

Chapter 2

- Recognition

Naturally, in an organization that lives and works by such principles, managers have a jump-start on the kind of supporting culture which is widely acknowledged to produce employee satisfaction and its logical result, employee retention.

Sweet feels that the journey to achieving agent satisfaction depends heavily on agents knowing what is expected of them, participating in the decisions around those expectations and the certainty that the organization's leadership will support them in achieving individual and company goals.

A CHECKLIST FOR POSITIVE AGENT DEVELOPMENT

- Set up a planned program of skills acquisition for agents as a regular part of on-the-job training. Reward them for each level of achievement.
- Hold lunch break seminars on any topic of interest. Ask in-house experts to share information on work-related and nonwork-related subjects. Get agents involved with planning and running the seminars.
- Provide Web-based training or computer-based training to improve customer service skills and/or knowledge sets.
- Provide tuition reimbursement for any outside course, whether or not it's related to work.
- Meet regularly with agents to share information on work-related issues, or to research and solve a problem that's been bugging you.
- Provide continuing education instruction in enterprise-related fields.
- Use your company's Web page or intranet to link to sites that relate to your business. Encourage agents to explore what's going on in your industry.
- Create a list of subject-matter experts in your organization—encourage agents to qualify to be on the list.
- Incent agents to share learning.

The Road to Agent Satisfaction

The journey on the road to agent satisfaction begins with managers and supervisors having a thorough understanding of the business unit which they support. This understanding drives consistency in the process of providing customer support.

Frequent communication and feedback loops ensure that agents know what's happening in the business unit and when, so they can be prepared for call volume spikes and new product information. In the Digital Products call center process, there is the opportunity for give-and-take on issues that affect the center's ability to handle customer traffic.

In addition, call center leaders must work with agents to establish goals, which should be clearly communicated to the entire call center.

Individual performance plans can then be developed for each agent, again, with their input. At Kodak, agents are measured on performance factors like call quality, training adherence and demonstration of company values in their customer interactions.

EMPLOYEE COMMITMENT FACTS

- *Training Magazine* points to two studies listing the keys to employee retention and loyalty. More pay is not included in the top-ranking factors.
- According to research by human resources consulting firm The Hay Group, the most important contributors to employee satisfaction are:

  The type of work 89%

  Respectful treatment 69%

  Coaching and feedback 64%

  Learning new skills 61%
- Aon Consulting of Chicago reported these top five reasons for employee satisfaction:
  1. Employer's recognition of personal and family time.
  2. The organization's vision and direction.
  3. Personal growth opportunities.
  4. The ability to challenge the way things are done.
  5. Everyday work satisfaction.

Chapter 2

Address Agent Development in a Positive Way

Kodak makes a strong commitment to supporting employee realization of individual goals. Fifty percent of every training dollar spent on employees goes toward fostering success on their current job, and the other half is spent on helping them to be successful in a future position.

Agents receive at least one hour of training every day before the call center opens. Individual coaching is also available. Sweet feels that this incredible level of commitment to continual learning contributes heavily to the high customer satisfaction ratings (97 percent), as well as to the low turnover rate.

Each team has a "sponsor" for every metric. That person is responsible for assuring that the metric is understood, measurements are taken and communicated and that additional coaching is available if needed.

Sweet feels that to have a high-performance work culture, companies are obligated to position their people so they can be successful. Her goal is to teach her agents to think, make decisions and act.

Chapter 2

Top Companies Take a Tactical Approach to Agent Satisfaction

by Susan Hash

In the early 1990s, Harvard Business School researched the direct and strong correlation between employee satisfaction, customer loyalty and profitability. They found that the organizations that consistently score high in customer satisfaction share a top-down concern for and focus on frontline employees. Their conclusion, referred to as the service-profit chain, has been instrumental in evolving corporate cultures over the past decade.

American Express Co. has been one of the forerunners of the service-profit chain concept, with a culture that is strongly focused on employee satisfaction.

Senior VP and Customer Champion Jim Blann is a firm believer in the link between employee satisfaction and customer satisfaction. "It's absolutely integral," he says. "I've talked to enough people in our servicing organization to know that our reps get a great feeling of satisfaction from doing a terrific job for the customer."

Beth Lacey, senior VP of Card Operations for American Express, agrees. "We support the whole notion of the service-profit chain, which is that satisfied employees lead to loyal customers—and that leads to improved shareholder performance."

Internet service provider EarthLink/MindSpring is another staunch supporter of that concept. The organization has received numerous top honors and awards for customer service and satisfaction. Carter Calle, executive VP of customer support, attributes much of that to the company's core values and belief in employee satisfaction as a foundation for customer satisfaction.

"If you satisfy the frontline reps who are the voice of the company, that translates into an improved customer experience and, therefore, improved customer satisfaction," Calle says.

Chapter 2

The Workforce Makeup Is Changing

Satisfied call center agents can increase customer satisfaction. But what increases agent satisfaction? A decade ago, many employee relationship consultants touted "warm, fuzzy" strategies managers should use to create a more pleasant working atmosphere for call center and customer service staff. Those included niceties and informal appreciation techniques, such as saying "hello" to every agent at the beginning of a shift, sending personalized thank-you notes for outstanding performance, impromptu pizza parties after heavy call volume periods, and casual-dress Fridays.

While those things are still important, the call center industry has grown and evolved—and with it, managers are finding the complexion of its workforce has changed, too.

Steve Sharkey has noticed an influx of younger candidates—with less work and life experience—into the call center environment. Sharkey is manager of Northern and Southern Inquiry Centers for Public Service Electric and Gas Company (PSE&G) in New Jersey. In the past, the utility's CSPs (customer service professionals) came to the call center after years of experience in other PSE&G departments. Now the average age of its CSPs is mid- to late-20s, with three to five years' service experience, Sharkey says. "This is basically just a 'way station' for them. They want to do a good job, and they want to move on to other areas of the company."

In many call centers today, the typical job candidate can no longer be considered a "lifer." Instead, they're interested in building a career that, most likely, will take them out of the center. A key satisfaction element for these career-minded employees revolves around training and development.

To meet those needs, PSE&G offers its CSPs additional personal training, such as courses in Microsoft programs like Word, Excel or PowerPoint.

Putting the Needs of the Agent First

Although the industry and its frontline employees have evolved significantly over the past years, some of the frustrations of the job are the same. A long-time frustration for frontline agents is not being able to answer callers' questions or resolve their problems on the spot.

EarthLink's philosophy is to put as much information as possible at the agents' fingertips so they don't get surprised by customers, says Calle. "We help them to be a knowledge expert on whatever topic the customer is calling about," he says. Agents have access to the accounting database to allow them to pull up a customer's specific billing history and other features of their accounts. They also have tools that allow them to view Web pages and pull email. "We try to give them everything they need to know and understand in order to help a customer," he says.

Calle says that he is sometimes questioned about the need for agents to access specific information, such as billing histories. But he stands by his agents' requests. "Never underestimate the value of your reps," he says. "If they say they need it, I'm not going to question them. If it's not a privacy issue, or a financial issue for the company, then we should make the information available. If it helps the reps to do their job, then it's going to help the customers."

It's the Information Age, So Let it Flow

Constant communication and updates are an important component of frontline support at American Express. Agents are kept informed in a variety of ways as new products or services are introduced, depending on the complexity of the announcement, says Lacey. "If it's very basic, they may get a flash [bulletin] as they sign on to their PCs at the start of their shift."

For more complex updates, such as system process changes, which agents need to understand how to execute, desktop simulations that agents can perform at their workstations may be used.

Before a new product is released, agents are taken off the phones to work with the marketing organization. "We want to make sure they understand what the product is, how we're going to be able to service it, and what types of questions customers may ask," Lacey says. "We explain the value story for each product or service to the agents so they can then share that with the customers."

American Express is currently formalizing a process to ensure agent input into marketing materials. Before any marketing communication goes out, the company conducts focus groups with agents. "They're a very rich source of information as to how customers may react or how they may understand what we're trying to communicate," Lacey says. "It's just another link in the chain of how employees can help to drive customer loyalty."

Giving the Frontline a Voice

Because the people, processes and technologies that comprise the call center environment is perpetually changing, keeping a handle on agent satisfaction requires continuous feedback and input from the front lines.

"In the call center, we measure how people are feeling about their environment on a quarterly basis," says American Express' Lacey. In addition, a formal companywide employee satisfaction survey is conducted annually.

Employee satisfaction is measured against 13 dimensions that are most correlated with delivering high-quality service, she says. Those include having the right tools to do the job, having training and development opportunities, having the appropriate amount of authority to solve customer issues, being valued for contributions to the company, being recognized and rewarded appropriately for their work, and working for people they can respect.

The organization compares its results against other top companies of similar size and with similar types of processes, but that are not necessarily in the financial industry. "We conduct the benchmarking research and identify a target point of arrival," Lacey says. "Then our efforts are focused on closing any gaps we have internally against that point of arrival."

Teams, which include frontline agents, are pulled together to concentrate on improving areas that fall below the benchmark before the next annual survey and review. They follow a structured process to identify the gaps and then develop implementation plans to improve performance.

In addition to quantitative results from the employee satisfaction surveys, the company values open-ended commentary from the front line, as well. "They're very useful in determining what our action plans should be," Lacey says.

And given the chance, frontline employees can be very honest and insightful with their feedback.

"There's a very strong orientation within our employee group to deliver great service to our customers," says American Express' Blann. "That's just part of our DNA as a company. And through this survey, we sometimes get feedback that policies we've created or processes that have evolved over time are getting in the way of delivering great service. So we use employee feedback to make the changes and remove the barriers so that our employees can do a better job for customers."

Managers Are Accountable for Frontline Satisfaction

Developing a customer-focused culture that recognizes employee satisfaction as a key contributor requires a top-down accountability. Employee satisfaction survey results are taken seriously by managers at American Express. Anyone in the organization who manages people—from team leaders up to the CEO—is rated on the employee satisfaction survey results. In fact, employee satisfaction accounts for 25 percent of a manager's performance goal and, consequently, compensation.

PSE&G has a formal Customer Relationship Measurement Process in place to ensure companywide visibility and accountability. One of its measurement components is a scorecard for managers which includes sections on employee engagement, customer relationships and profitability. Part of call center management's performance incentives are based on the center's performance in meeting both the business and human needs of customers. Human needs include having interactions with agents who show empathy, are courteous and respectful, and demonstrate interest and concern for the customer's issues.

Don't Undervalue the Impact of Good Will

However, numbers aside, the top goal for the 15 supervisors and team leaders at PSE&G's Northern and Southern call centers is to build good will, says

21

Sharkey. "I believe that if you build good will, everything else ensues, even profitability."

The utility's supervisors and team leaders keep notes or logs describing their good will performance—individuals they've helped in some way by giving extra coaching attention, giving someone a few hours off to take care of personal business or lending an ear when someone is having difficulties. Recently, a couple of supervisors arranged for half of their team, about 15 people, to attend a morning funeral for a colleague who lost his son. The impact of that kind of support was felt departmentwide.

"I feel comfortable that we have the measurements that we need in place," Sharkey says. "Yet all of that is for naught if you don't know the people and you don't understand what the issues are beyond schedule adherence and call-handling."

Michelle Soto, team leader at PSE&G's Northern Inquiry Center, agrees. "You can see the rapport between the supervisors and the employees—and that, in itself, creates high productivity levels," she says. "We just came through a very stressful few months preparing a contingency plan for work stoppage and renegotiating a union contract, but you would never know it walking around the center."

AmeriCredit: Strong Focus on Values Promotes Positive Team Culture
by Susan Hash

There's no doubt that a positive call center culture fosters agent retention, higher performance and customer satisfaction. In fact, a strong culture acts as the foundation upon which other processes can be built, such as career development, service quality, monitoring and coaching.

Call centers have long suffered from a negative workplace image due to inflexible rules, a focus on quantitative measures, heavy supervision, relentless call volumes and feelings of powerlessness among agents. Historically, culture problems have been further exacerbated by the organization's negative view of the call center and a lack of solid leadership.

Yet there are exceptions. One organization that "walks the talk" with regard to its mission, culture and values is AmeriCredit Corp., a national consumer finance company that specializes in purchasing and servicing automobile loans, headquartered in Fort Worth, Texas. The organization has about 4,500 employees throughout North America, and five call center sites.

What is it that makes AmeriCredit's culture unique? It begins with a clearly defined mission statement and values—but it doesn't end there.

"Many corporations will have statements up on the wall and they'll tell you what they're about—but when you meet the employees and get into the environment, you don't see those types of attributes displayed," says Vice President of Customer Service Alicia M. Gadley.

"We strive for a true balance of worklife, culture, profitability and productivity," agrees Lori Whitney, senior vice president of customer service. "And what's different about AmeriCredit—this company lives its values."

One crucial proof of living the values is in the way the call center measures agent performance. "Our focus is on being available for the customer," explains Gadley. "Instead of measuring average handle time or talk time, we measure the availability of the CSR for the customer. And if they're not available for the cus-

Chapter 2

AMERICREDIT'S MISSION AND VALUES

AmeriCredit's mission is to create value for our stakeholders by constantly improving our services, investing in innovative solutions and information-based strategies, and promoting a culture of teamwork, excellence and integrity.

AmeriCredit's i4 Values

Four words in this statement are so meaningful that, when brought together, their magnitude is raised to the fourth power.

Integrity: Character and respect shall govern our actions. Treat others the way you expect to be treated and lead by example. Value our stakeholders' opinions and actively listen to ensure we understand their views and deliver what we promise with loyalty to execution.

Investment: Attract, motivate and retain outstanding employees by investing in their welfare and development. Build mutually beneficial relationships to provide best-in-class customer service. Champion transfer of knowledge and encourage people to become resources to each other. Participate as a partner in the community.

Innovation: Never become complacent. Embrace change and participate in exploring opportunities to improve. Proactively create our future by challenging the status quo and daring to innovate. Commit to realizing efficiency gains and the benefits of continual improvement.

Information: Share information and promote open communication. Encourage everyone to participate in a non-intimidation environment. Develop and deploy our strategies and measure performance using all available technology.

AmeriCredit Statement of Values

AmeriCredit is a workplace where dedicated people have the opportunity to work together and celebrate our successes. Our people care about each other, listen to and respect ideas, leave egos at the door—because they have no place here—and champion teamwork. For the privilege of playing on this team, we practice and protect these principles with utmost sincerity.

tomer, then we look at what types of things they're doing to get a better picture of any roadblocks we may need to remove."

Reinforcing the Mission and Values

In addition to visibly displaying the mission statement at the various sites, the company's i4 values (see box on page 24) are continuously reinforced, says Whitney. Employees are first introduced to the company's values during new-hire orientation videos and a CEO-hosted luncheon. New-hires are also given wallet-sized cards printed with the mission, i4 values and statement of values.

As an organization, AmeriCredit is serious about maintaining the culture and values it has developed—so much so, it has created an executive position to oversee it. Senior Vice President of Corporate Culture Debbie Diamond leads a group whose role is to help keep the organization focused on its corporate culture, and ensure that all processes and programs are aligned with it. In her role, she also serves as an internal consultant to advise the executive team on employee investments, and initiates projects to keep the culture strong.

One way is through collecting constant feedback from AmeriCredit team members (employees). "We have a variety of listening tools that we use to monitor how we're doing with living our culture internally," she says.

One listening tool is an annual i4 survey. It's an in-depth online survey with some 65 statements that describe the company's expectations with regard to behaviors for living the culture, which team members are asked to rate. "We also give them an opportunity to share their ideas to enhance the culture," says Diamond. And in fact, many of the processes in place today are a result of employee feedback from i4 surveys.

Each year, the company also holds Town Hall meetings—attended by every employee—in which members of the executive team and human resources go out to the various operational sites to give updates on what's going on in the company, and what's happening with their particular business units, as well as to give team members an opportunity to ask questions and get answers on the spot.

Chapter 2

Other listening tools include periodic focus groups, additional surveys (such as a work/life balance survey) and benchmarking against top companies.

A Focus on Staff Development

A positive culture cannot exist without growth opportunities. Call center leaders at AmeriCredit put together individual action plans for each team member that allows them to either build on the skills they have to be more effective or to grow their careers, says Gadley.

"We have some individuals who don't want a leadership role; they want to be the best they can be at the CSR level. So we've put training in place to help them achieve their goals. We also have individuals who want a career path within the department, so we work with them on action plans to enhance the skills they need to progress through the different levels."

Besides training within the call center, agents can take advantage of the organization's leadership and team member development program, which includes a series of leadership modules grouped into four core areas: leadership skills, personal development, team dynamics and human resource management, as well as a team member investment component that focuses on the workplace environment (e.g., adapting to change, dealing with workplace conflict) and personal development (e.g., listening skills, stress management, time management, communicating effectively, etc.).

Recognizing Team Members

Regular appreciation and recognition of employees are also fundamental components of a solid culture. And AmeriCredit makes use of companywide opportunities for recognition, as well as supporting various programs within each department.

Recently, the organization launched three companywide recognition tools (as a result from last year's i4 survey):

- **iCard**—organizationwide recognition. An iCard is an electronic "card" that any team member in the organization can send to any other team member or team to show appreciation for going above and beyond. "The recipient receives an electronic copy as well as a hard copy he or she can post in the work area that specifically describes what he or she did to deserve this recognition," says Diamond. The recipient's supervisor also receives a copy. Each quarter, all iCard recipients are automatically entered in a drawing for a shopping spree at a special Web site that contains AmeriCredit logo products.

- **iAwards**—superior-to-subordinate recognition. AmeriCredit leaders can recognize sustained or extraordinary performance by a team member or a team by bestowing an iAward. Recipients receive credits that they can use for shopping on the company products Web site.

- **iClub**—a quarterly organizationwide award. With iClub awards, any team member can nominate any other team member or a group of people in the company for above-and-beyond performance in which results far exceed expectations. Nominations are reviewed by a group of officers, and recipients receive cash awards.

In addition to the corporate recognition efforts, individual sites and departments have their own recognition programs. For instance, the customer service department participates in several, such as:

- An internal recognition program. Each month team members can nominate individuals who they feel have demonstrated one or more of the i4 values. Nominators submit a recognition form describing (in 50 words or more) why or how a particular individual has displayed the i4 values. A committee of CSRs, team leaders and account managers, reviews the recommendation forms and selects a winner each month. That individual receives a plaque and a $50 gift certificate. Winners' names go on the Wall of Fame in gold, and at the end of the year, all i4 winners are invited to a special recognition luncheon.

- Monthly team events. A special activities committee comes up with monthly festivities designed to boost morale, typically involving food, decorations and holiday celebrations.

- A team recognition program. Each customer service team is allotted $50 per month. Together, team members decide if they want to recognize the entire

Chapter 2

team or individuals within the team, and how.

- An internal newsletter. "The employees have put together a wonderful newsletter that focuses on the personal side of the department, as well as the business side," says Whitney.

CSR Involvement in the Center

AmeriCredit's frontline CSRs are actively involved in helping to develop their department's processes and procedures. "We try to ensure that we have an all-inclusive environment," says Gadley. "It's very important that we have feedback and input from everyone within the environment." For instance, customer service staff helped to develop the call monitoring form, and several individuals also work with a quality team to conduct the monitoring.

CSRs are currently on committees charged with developing an attendance policy and performance evaluation processes. Also, a special process improvement team was put together recently to review specific processes that affect customers and the customer value chain from beginning to end.

"We've provided them with organizational development and facilitation training. We're also involving staff from different functional and geographical centers," says Whitney. "They've got a task that requires a lot of responsibility and accountability."

Investing in the Community

Besides investing in its employees, AmeriCredit encourages its employees to invest in their communities. "Investment is one of our core values," says Diamond.

Employees are fully supported for taking part in community or volunteer activities. In fact, each employee gets eight hours of paid time off per quarter to participate in company-sponsored charities or in a charity of their choice.

AmeriCredit has four annual signature events that are sponsored throughout North America: the United Way, Susan G. Komen Breast Cancer Foundation, Salvation Army and March of Dimes. At these events, departments help to raise

TIPS FOR BUILDING A POSITIVE CULTURE

Following are suggestions for developing a positive culture from Ann Smith, president of AG Smith & Associates, a Dallas, Texas-based consulting firm specializing in call center technology and management (www.agsmithconsulting.com).

- Understand your organization's operating model. Many managers may know what needs to be done to cultivate a positive culture, but often find themselves swimming against the current because they aren't working within the framework for their specific company. For example, if your environment is a "command-and-control" type, the way you approach selling a program to enhance the culture will be very different than in a more empowered center.
- Begin with a change strategy. First things first: If change management is a sketch topic for you, do the research to learn more about it. It will make your job easier and help you to avoid potential mistakes later.
- Identify and document the most important aspects of your desired culture. Be absolutely certain the intent and reach of these goals are clearly defined. Leave no opportunity for misunderstanding. For example, a phrase such as "fair treatment" is sure to be interpreted differently by various individuals.
- Align everything you say and do with your culture goals. While the steps to ensure that concrete processes (such as compensation, departmental policies, etc.) parallel culture goals will be more clear-cut, it's the day-to-day demonstration of commitment and alignment that establishes a culture. For instance, soliciting employee feedback, yet never following through on their suggestions and input sends a contrary message to staff.
- Work to ensure that trust is the cornerstone of your culture. Build trust through honest communication and delivering on promises. Living the culture on a daily basis solidifies trust.
- Tap into the power of your people! Whatever you call it—buy-in, discipleship, engagement—keep in mind, it quickly spreads throughout an organization. Call center managers who have experienced this phenomenon negatively at some point know the power—so use it to your center's advantage.

Chapter 2

money through bake sales, dunk tanks, contests, etc., which the company then matches dollar for dollar, says Diamond.

Another contribution program is Dollars for Doers. If an employee volunteers 20 to 50 hours of his or her time per year to a specific organization, the company will make a $5 per hour contribution to that charity in that employee's name.

Team members also can be sponsored by the company in two run/walk events of their choosing per year. In addition, the company responded to the September 11 tragedies with a $100,000 contribution to the Red Cross, and team members made an additional contribution of $50,000. "It's a very caring group of people," says Diamond.

Elements of a Successful Culture

Is the focus on culture and values making a difference at AmeriCredit? If the results from the last i4 survey are any indication, then it would seem so. Employee feedback on the company's performance is very positive—ranking AmeriCredit higher than other top-performing companies in 27 of 29 specific areas. In addition, staff turnover has dropped from 37 percent in 1999 to 21 percent in 2001. At the same time, the employee population more than doubled from 2,000 to 4,500.

Diamond attributes the success of the culture to believing in and meeting the values on a day-to-day basis.

"You can't just post the words on a wall or increase the benefits and assume the culture will improve," she says. "If there isn't good communication on a daily basis in the environment, if people don't feel that they have a clear path, and if people don't feel that there is workplace balance, then all of the hoopla and parties will mean nothing. The foundation has to be the relationship, the communication and the trust."

Create a Pleasant, Productive Environment that Will Boost Agent Retention

by Roger Kingsland

"We like working here." What call center manager wouldn't want to hear those four words coming from more of his or her agents? What value would that bring to your operation?

The integration of online technologies with traditional voice-based customer interaction presents new challenges to get agents better trained in a wider range of support services. But as the economy stalls, call center managers are also increasingly confronted with corporate mandates to cut costs while improving productivity and efficiency. Most are being asked to do more with less—and that's not an easy task to accomplish.

Customers, meanwhile, are ever more sophisticated in their buying patterns and expectations for fast, quality service. They want the voice on the other end of the phone line to be knowledgeable and pleasant; they want their orders placed or inquiries answered quickly—and they're not in the mood to wait.

Against that backdrop, the chronic crisis of turnover among the rank-and-file call center workers—with all the resulting increased costs of disruption, service inconsistencies and new staff training—has taken on a new sense of urgency. Savvy call center managers recognize that helping their employees more fully enjoy their time at work is not an expendable soft issue—it's a bottomline imperative.

So how can you make the work experience more pleasant and rewarding for your agents in a way that will reduce turnover, improve productivity and enhance the bottom line?

Logically enough, the process should really start at the beginning of the call center's existence—with the initial architectural design or renovation plan. Decisions made then can have a lasting impact on employee morale, and thus financial performance, throughout the life of the call center.

Chapter 2

31

Call Centers Are Not Typical Office Space

All too often, corporate management fails to recognize the vast differences between call centers and conventional office space. Call centers have almost double the occupation density of typical offices, and they tend to operate longer hours—many are now in operation 24-hours, seven days a week.

Workloads and staffing can vary greatly from hour to hour. Call centers also require a substantial (and potentially intrusive) technology infrastructure that can be in constant flux as new systems are developed and new processes deployed, all the while ensuring the sustainability of the technology through foolproof generation systems, uninterrupted power supplies and disaster-recovery planning.

Call center design is more than envisioning what the finished product may look like when construction is completed. It's about planning for the unknowns of call volumes and new technologies that might develop further down the road. It's about expecting the unexpected, which requires a unique approach to call center design and/or renovation—one that emphasizes flexibility and adaptability.

FUTURE-PROOF YOUR CALL CENTER

As we move further into the multichannel, highly networked economy, successful knowledge-based organizations must have the ability to change quickly and efficiently in order to survive. Call centers, in particular, must also have the ability to change at the "speed of business."

The best way to future-proof your call center is to allow for substantially more layout flexibility than is typical today. Components that should be considered include:

- Uniform, ceiling-mounted indirect lighting systems that are layout independent.
- Furniture on wheels or furniture systems that can be reconfigured overnight.
- Raised floors that allow ultimate cabling flexibility.

Consider the Agents' View (Literally)

The call center industry is rife with design decision-making that's based on expediency and short-term cost considerations—and disregards the long-range perspective that is required. For instance, cutting capital costs typically is seen as the best, if not only, way to add value to a call center project. In situations where call center workers are paid poorly and possess relatively low skill sets, management often perceives little or no justification for a thoughtful approach. In these types of call centers, the consequences of high turnover are considered an unavoidable by-product of pay and status, or of the nature of the workers who are attracted to the job.

Call center design often reflects a corporate hierarchy that is not appropriate to the realities of the situation. For example, many call centers have more private offices than are necessary. Also, those offices are generally located along the outside walls where they steal the natural light. Call center staff too often are relegated to noisy, stark break rooms dominated by vending machines and trash cans.

Please don't misconstrue the point here. No one is suggesting that executives should be penalized for their positions within a call center. The argument is that executive perquisites need not be at the expense of building a pleasant, nurturing environment that gives agents a reason to more fully enjoy their jobs and stick with them.

In other words, short-term decision-making need not be the rule.

Design Issues to Consider

There is a growing body of research that proves a phenomenal performance connection between employee-centered design and improved productivity, efficiencies and return on investment. We can now accurately pinpoint how investments in areas such as ergonomics, spatial dynamics, site amenities, furniture, lighting, acoustics and heating, ventilation and air conditioning systems and others can pay off.

Following are just a few of the issues you might want to consider in the design decision-making process.

- **Workstations.** All of us have a basic psychological need for personal space and some degree of privacy—even in a crowded, busy call center. Simple solutions include the placing of workstations in a non-fixed, varied pattern and providing each with storage space for personal belongings.

- **Break rooms.** Typically, break rooms tend to be unpleasant places. An alternative is to create a centrally located "community center" with conference

---

MAKE A BUSINESS CASE FOR RENOVATIONS

Once the components of good call center design are understood, the next step is to make a business case for incorporating them into the design solution. An excellent example is ergonomics. As most managers have become aware over the past decade, the cost to provide good ergonomic support is miniscule compared to the benefits. The example below illustrates the potential for savings. For this example, let's assume a 10 percent productivity increase for a call center using ergonomically designed furniture. (Estimate taken from a study by Springer Associates Inc. that concluded ergonomic furniture resulted in a 10-15 percent performance improvement over normal conditions.)

Equipment/furniture costs

Chair...$550
Adjustable monitor stand....................$30
Adjustable keyboard.........................$120
Footrest $50
Total..$750
.....................................(Round to $1,000)

ROI calculation

a. Cost of improvements (from above) =...$1,000/agent
b. Debt service to borrow cost of improvements
   (assume 9.5% over 5 years) = ...$252/agent/year
c. Average direct personnel expense (DPE*) =..........................$20,000/agent/year
d. Productivity increase = ...10%
e. DPE savings due to productivity increase
   [(c) x d) / 100] =..$2,000/agent/year
f. Return on investment [(e)/(b)] =..793%

* Salary plus benefits

---

rooms, human resources offices, reading tables and other amenities. Lighting should be diffused and subtle. Some companies even include kitchen and/or daycare facilities.

- **Color.** Use a color scheme that reduces stress and maintains suitable brightness levels, with accent colors and lighting that adds interest and variety. For instance, painting over drab gray walls with cool bluish-green hues has been shown to have a calming affect on agents while enhancing mental alertness.

- **Exposed ceilings.** Higher ceilings can add to a person's sense of spatial freedom. You can achieve higher ceilings through exposed structural systems.

- **Indirect lighting.** Indirect lighting shines up to the ceiling and then reflects back down onto the work surface. It is ideally suited for computer-intensive environments because it provides an appropriate contrast with the computer screen.

- **Integrated-access floor systems.** Raised-access (computer) floors are often installed in call centers so that modular power, data and communications cables can be located in the floor cavity. A fully integrated solution would include environmental air supplied through that cavity, as well. Not only can cabling changes be made at lower cost, but the vertical flow of air from floor to ceiling improves overall air quality. Floor registers also can be installed or moved to give individuals the ability to change the air temperature in their immediate vicinity.

- **Noise reduction.** Excessive noise is a leading cause of employee dissatisfaction with the call center work environment. The higher density of bodies in call centers, as well as the lower furniture panel heights used, compound the noise problem. Sound-masking systems reduce noise by emitting a frequency from ceiling speakers that mask the sounds of human voices.

Modest Investments Create a Call Center to Boast about

Relatively modest investments made during a call center design process can return significant benefits during the life of the center. The challenge for call center management is to push for the right decisions, even at the risk of slightly higher upfront costs. Architectural design firms can help you to quantify the rewards and ROI those investments would generate.

After all, when it comes to your call center's bottom line, it really does matter if your employees say, "We like working here."

Chapter 2

Chapter 3: Enhance Agent Retention

Companies have been battling agent attrition since the dawn of call centers. The good news is that, after years of trial-and-error, effective practices have emerged for attracting qualified staff, gaining their commitment, and inspiring them to grow within the organization.

Key Aspects of Successful Agent Retention Processes

by Greg Levin

Call centers are hemorrhaging staff as never before. Typical call center attrition rates fall between the 30 percent to 50 percent range, with rates over 100 percent not at all unheard of.

In recent years, many companies have claimed a renewed focus on and respect of call center staff, but the mass agent-exodus—and the exorbitant costs associated with it—continues. Why?

"I really don't think that the majority of call center managers focus on what needs to be done to improve agent retention," says Laura Sikorski, managing partner of consulting firm Sikorski-Tuerpe & Associates. "They go through the motions of conducting 'exit interviews' with all the agents who decide to leave, but they don't do anything with the information they gather. They seem to have bought into the myth that high turnover is inevitable in the call center environment."

And that's a costly myth to buy into—especially today, with added pressures on call centers and agents to effectively handle an ever-increasing and more demanding customer base using a wide range of contact channels.

Call Center Management Review scanned the entire industry to pinpoint the key factors associated with high staff retention. Let's take a look at some of those, with examples of call centers that are doing innovative things in specific areas.

Fair and Creative Compensation

Like anybody in the job market, agents want to be paid not just a competitive wage, but one that reflects the value of their skill, effort and impact on their specific organization.

"We're asking agents to know more, to compile and manage more customer

Chapter 3

41

STUDY IDENTIFIES FACTORS IMPACTING CALL CENTER CULTURE

Call center culture has a direct impact on agent retention, as well as productivity, service delivery and financial success, according to *Call Center Culture: The Hidden Success Factor in Achieving Service Excellence*, a study by The Radclyffe Group. The study surveyed nearly 1,500 agents and managers in more than a dozen industries to identify the issues that make working in a call center so challenging.

Four factors impact culture

The study found that there are four common factors within call centers that impact the culture or the way agents feel about their jobs:

1. The rules are perceived as stringent and inflexible.

2. The work is stressful by nature.

3. Call centers tend to assess overall performance using quantitative measures.

4. Schedules and phone time are managed in the moment.

Key differentiators of positive culture

The study found that, in those call centers in which a negative culture exists, 70 percent of respondents say that the key differentiators to positive culture are missing. Those are: effective communication, professional development, employee job satisfaction and trust.

- **Effective communication.** In centers that ranked high for positive culture, just under 70 percent reported that the flow of communication within the organization is open and direct, compared with 46 percent in the middle responding companies and only 30 percent reported by the bottom five companies.

- **Professional development.** Only 19 percent of employees in call centers with negative cultures agree that they receive timely feedback for improving their performance.

- **Employee satisfaction.** Nearly 80 percent of respondents say their call center does not encourage them to do their best.

- **Trust.** Only 14 percent of respondents agree that people trust each other in their call centers.

> The study also identified specific success factors that were found to contribute to positive call center culture. Those included: agents being proud to work in the organization; having a strong sense of identity within the company; and receiving the direction, training and feedback necessary to do their jobs well and to be successful.
>
> *Source: The Radclyffe Group, 973-276-0522; Web site www.radclyffegroup.com*

data, to be generalist and specialists, and to upsell and cross-sell, yet the industry has depressed agents' wages because it still insists on viewing the job as entry level," says Mary Beth Ingram, president of call center training firm Phone Pro.

Many of the best-managed call centers not only pay agents a decent starting wage, they've also implemented skills-based pay programs that enable agents to earn additional pay as they attain more advanced skills and knowledge. For example, one U.S. pet supply company starts its customer service agents off at an ample $24,000 a year and gives them the opportunity to earn up to $35,000 if they complete all 20 modules of the center's "skills ladder." One of the center's supervisors says that the starting salary and skills-based pay opportunities play a big part in maintaining the call center's 92 percent agent retention rate.

"People here don't look at the call center as merely a place to *begin* a career, but as a place to *have* a career," says the supervisor. She adds that the center's compensation approach not only helps to retain quality staff, it helps to attract a diverse group of quality applicants when the center is hiring; 19 different college degrees are represented among the center's 35 agents.

Incentives and Recognition

While money can be a strong motivator, agents need additional enticements and encouragement to perform in what can be a very challenging environment, as well as recognition whenever they do perform well.

Chapter 3

Effective incentive programs and recognition practices needn't require a significant financial investment. True, cash bonuses and large gift certificates make nice rewards for contest winners, but so do paid time off, recognition in company newsletters, trophies/plaques and time off the phones to work on special projects.

Call centers with the most successful incentive programs offer a mix of monetary and non-monetary awards that are based on both quality and productivity measurements. And they recognize both individual and team or centerwide achievement.

Call centers focused on staff retention involve agents in the development and maintenance of the incentive programs, either by asking them for feedback on what type of rewards they prefer or, as in the case of Air Canada, by letting agents run the show. Air Canada's Vancouver call center implemented an agent-led incentive program in 1996 to empower staff and enhance motivation and retention. Leading the program is a six-agent Incentive Committee that creates and promotes each contest and decides on the prizes awarded, such as gift certificates to hotels, restaurants, movie theaters and retail stores. "Agents have their fingers on the pulse of our center, so they are the natural people to create incentives for everyone," says manager Butch Gregoire.

Other call centers encourage agents to recognize each other's accomplishments. For example, mail order cataloger JD Williams in Manchester, England, sponsors a monthly "Flair Award," in which agents nominate peers who demonstrate outstanding performance.

Project Involvement and Decision-Making

One of the best—and easiest—ways to enhance the overall image of the agent position and improve retention is to actively involve agents in a variety of important projects, processes and decisions in the call center. Smart call centers are tapping the talent and energy of their agents to enhance such crucial areas as hiring, training, monitoring and, as mentioned earlier in the Air Canada example, incentives/recognition.

Chapter 3

Mentoring programs—where veteran agents pair up with new-hires to help guide them through initial training and/or their first days handling calls—have become increasingly popular. For example, trainees at Today's Merchandising's call center in Peoria, Ill., are partnered with experienced agents for nearly a month before going solo on the phones. Since introducing its "New Employee Partners" program in 1996, the call center has seen a significant reduction in turnover—for both new-hires and experienced agents—and an increase in overall performance and morale.

Peer monitoring programs—where agents evaluate each other's calls and pro-

---

HEALTHY AGENTS WORK BETTER, STAY LONGER

It's difficult to achieve healthy service levels and customer loyalty without healthy agents. Commitment to effective call center design/ergonomics and stress-reduction practices can have a tremendous impact on staff performance, morale and retention.

That's exactly what Wisconsin Power and Light (a division of Alliant Energy) was thinking when it introduced its "Keep Well" program at its Janesville, Wis., call center several years ago. In addition to providing all agents with ample 7x7 foot cubicles equipped with ergonomically advanced chairs, footrests/armrests and electric workstation tabletops (so that each workstation can be adjusted to the proper height), the center brings in an occupational therapist to work with each new training class. The therapist shows each new-hire how to adjust his or her equipment and position his or her body to avoid Cumulative Trauma Disorder (CTS).

The company also contracts with a massage therapist to work on tense agents during the peak season (April-October). In addition, the call center has "quiet rooms"—equipped with comfortable couches/recliners, books and CD players—where agents can retreat when things get hectic. One room even has three exercise machines for agents who want to pedal or jog away their tension.

The company's investment has paid off. Since introducing the "Keep Well" program, agent absenteeism and turnover have dropped while productivity has risen.

vide constructive feedback—are also starting to take off in call centers. Not only does peer monitoring empower agents to enhance quality in the call center and learn valuable coaching skills, it helps to reduce agents' fear of and resistance to call monitoring in general. Most call centers with effective peer monitoring programs, such as Lands' End in Cross Plains, Wis., use the program to supplement the center's supervisor-led call monitoring methods.

Nobody knows the agent job—and what it takes to succeed in that job—like a call center's existing agents. That's why more and more centers are involving agents in the hiring process. The benefits of such an approach can be twofold: Turnover among existing agents drops because they see that the company respects their opinions and job knowledge; and turnover among new-hires drops because experienced agents help to enhance the selection process. A study by call center consulting firm Response Design Corp. indicated that, when centers include existing agents in the hiring process, new-hires are better matched with the company culture, begin the job with a clear understanding of their roles and responsibilities, and more quickly form bonds with coworkers.

Transition Training

Much of the turnover that rattles call centers occurs among new-hires. Even centers that offer weeks of training often lose agents early on because the agents are ill-prepared for the challenging and fast-paced world that awaits them on the phones.

Many call centers have stemmed early turnover by implementing some form of a "transition training" program, where new-hires who've completed or nearly completed adequate initial training begin handling basic customer calls in an "incubator" while under close supervision. In such a nurturing environment, new agents develop the confidence and skills they need to succeed on the regular phone floor, and thus are less likely to end their call center career early due to fear and frustration.

Toyota Financial Service's customer service center—which boasts a mere 10 percent agent attrition rate—credits its in-depth transition training with helping to significantly bolster retention. Following a two-week initial training program, new-hires at the call center in Cedar Rapids, Iowa, participate in the two-week transition program, where they handle basic call types (i.e., billing questions) in a separate "transition bay." A trainer and several coaches support, monitor and provide feedback to trainees, who then head back to the classroom for three more weeks of training. Once that is completed, trainees return to the transition bay to practice handling more complex call types until they are ready to work on the main phone floor.

While such extensive training programs require time and capital investment, the pay-off can be extraordinary. "Yes, there are costs associated with lengthening the overall training process," says Dan Lowe, a consultant who has worked closely with Toyota and other call centers that have implemented transition programs. "But consider the costs of *not* implementing a transition program, [particularly] the costs of rehiring and retraining due to high agent turnover."

Agent Development and Advancement

Most call centers spend too much time obsessing over customer relationship management and not enough time on *agent* relationship management. While nurturing customers and maximizing their value is important, it mustn't overshadow the importance of developing powerful and lucrative relationships with frontline staff members.

Arrowhead Water's call center in Brea, Calif., has implemented a formal "Leadership Program" to enhance agent career opportunities and retention. The two-year program is open to any agent who has worked in the center and performed well for at least a year. Agents who are selected for the program learn the details of each call center job and work on a variety of projects that test agents' initiative, time management skills and creativity. As they progress through the program, agents spend less time on the phones and more time working on projects, receiving occasional pay increases as they advance.

After completing the program, agents become eligible for frontline supervisory and other positions in the call center. "We're showing people that they don't have to go elsewhere to grow," says Jim Maguire, manager of the center.

Some call centers—particularly smaller ones—may not have the luxury of implementing a formal career path for agents. In such centers, agent "certification" and skills-based pay programs enable agents to "move up" in the call center while remaining on the phones to handle valuable customers.

Pitney Bowes' Mailing Systems Division has a skills-based pay program in place at its call centers that features 50 skill blocks divided into three categories: 1) core, 2) advanced, and 3) expert. Once an agent completes the training module for a particular skill block, he or she takes a written certification test on that skill block. Those who pass the test are deemed "certified" in that skill, and a specific dollar amount is added to their base salary.

"We have more control over our future now," says Joney Ashley, an agent at Pitney Bowes' call center in Spokane, Wash. "If you know the plan up front and you know there are opportunities, you're more inclined to stay at the company."

Fair and Attainable Performance Objectives

The simple act of determining your center's service level goals—and how you go about measuring agents' success in meeting those goals—has a huge influence on how long staff will stay in the call center. Too many call centers—often with pressure from upper management to cut operating costs—set unattainable performance objectives that set up agents for frustration and failure, and set up the call center for poor retention and customer loyalty.

One call center, Rodale Books in Emmaus, Pa., has created what it calls a "relationship-based" environment, where call center statistics are practically ignored. Instead, agent and centerwide performance are measured using a formal quality program that incorporates monitoring scores and customer survey results.

"We don't count things like number of calls answered per hour," says Jeanne Dorney, manager of customer service for Rodale and winner of the 1998 U.S. Call Center Manager of the Year award. "We look at how well agents do their job and how the customers perceive the service."

Dorney made the move from a mere transaction-based environment to a more relationship-based one after agents told her that they felt micromanaged. Once she found out how her staff felt, Dorney created a unique "declaration of independence," which lists specific goals that agents strive for independently and a pledge from management to focus less on the daily task sheet that agents complete each day.

Create Agent Careers

The call center has evolved rapidly in recent years and has the potential to become a powerful entity within the enterprise. But this will not happen until the call center's own agents develop the desire to launch the center to that level.

To create ambition and dedication among staff, companies must show them that they are key players and reward them accordingly. Agents are much less likely to leave if they perceive that they have a career, not a job.

"For many people, the agent profession could be such a wonderful, long-term career opportunity full of pride and satisfaction," says Phone Pro's Ingram, "But corporations haven't done enough to put the call center or the agent position in that light. It's a matter of equitable compensation, providing fulfilling opportunities and valuing people. It's so damn simple!"

Build Long-Term Loyalty from the Agent's Perspective

by Barbara Bauer

Agent turnover is costly and, for call centers, the expenses associated with replacing agents doesn't show any signs of slowing.

To tackle staff attrition head on, managers must search for creative solutions to keep skilled agents happy and continuously growing on the job. Whatever programs you put in place to develop and retain agents, it's important to consider frontline wants and needs from their perspective.

Look at the Basics: Pay and Appreciation

Let's face it, corporations can no longer sit back and expect employees to be loyal. There are lots of jobs available and most people expect to work for five to seven companies in a lifetime. So what can you do to cultivate loyalty in your call center?

First, look at compensation. Good employees expect to be paid a salary that's perceived to be at or above the market standards for the position. Note the key word: Perceived. It doesn't matter if the salary is above market if your agents believe they're not paid fairly. Check industry studies as well as the Bureau of Labor Statistics to compare salary ranges. If your center is on target, share this information with your agents. If not, you need to review and adjust your compensation plan.

Building agent loyalty starts with salary, but it doesn't end there. While some employees leave for more money, most people change jobs for other reasons. Even well-paid agents won't stay on the job if they feel unappreciated, don't like their supervisors or think the company doesn't care about them. Knowing what your agents want and need is crucial.

Measure Job-Fit Before Hiring

In general, there are four things employees want: 1) interesting work, 2) an opportunity for advancement, 3) feedback, and 4) work-life balance. Here again, perception is important. You may feel your call center provides these things, but do your agents feel similarly? Do potential candidates think you provide these things? If you hire the right person for the job—looking closely at the personality traits needed for success on the job—they will. It's called job-fit.

Some call center managers are still using the traditional hiring approach: relying on the resume and interviews, considering only the applicant's education and work experience. Instead, learn how to hire the person, not the qualifications. Gone are the days when a warm body with a high school diploma could fill a call center seat.

Today the focus should be on the candidate's abilities and traits—what it takes to do the job. For instance, call center agents need to be problem-solvers and good communicators with the ability to handle complex calls and transactions, as well as have a certain degree of "sit-ability" and stamina. You can teach the skills, but you can't teach traits or job-fit.

The best way to "see" the person behind the resume and interview is to profile candidates. Quite different from skills or honesty tests, personality profiling is an easy, non-threatening, unbiased way to discover the wants, needs and motivators of your potential hire.

There are a variety of validated, cost-effective tools on the market. Some have created a "benchmark" or target personality for call center agents. This target personality is based on the traits identified in successful agents. Keep in mind, benchmarks are different for inbound and outbound agents, as well as for sales and service agents, so look for a profiling company that differentiates among these agent types.

Profiling also has become an increasingly popular way to learn what motivates top-performing agents to consistently go above-and-beyond and develop new skills, as well as what prompts others to walk out the door.

Chapter 3

Build Skill-Development Paths

Nearly every high-performing agent wants opportunities to grow and advance. After you've developed a process for hiring top-notch agents, you'll need to put programs in place to retain them.

A common obstacle to career development programs in many call centers is limited opportunities to move up the corporate ladder. Even if this is the case in your center, you can still build development programs that retain and motivate your employees.

Traditional career paths have evolved into skill paths. For some agents, growth opportunities may include additional computer training; for others, it may mean opportunities to improve communication skills or to learn supervisory skills.

In addition to skills acquisition, you may have agents who view advancement as a chance to tackle new responsibilities and tasks. You can broaden and expand their opportunities with short-term, off-phone projects, such as involvement in companywide events or campaigns.

And, of course, there are still those who view advancement strictly as a matter of income growth and position title. The first step is to determine how your agents define advancement.

Communication Is Key

Along with opportunities to build skills and/or advance comes the need for performance feedback. Remember, though, that feedback is more than a few comments made during an annual performance review. Feedback includes rewarding staff for a job well done and recognizing extra effort.

To be effective at offering feedback, keep in mind that how you provide it is as important as what you say. Try to adapt the feedback you offer to the individual agent. For instance, your outgoing, enthusiastic and persuasive agents generally respond to public praise and recognition. Staff with this personality trait relish the spotlight and will strive to achieve it.

But with more reserved, analytical agents, it's best to provide clear, specific, job-relevant feedback. People with these traits are encouraged by specific, constructive criticism, as long as comments related to the job are shared in a private conversation or memo.

To keep your star call center agents productive, happy and growing, take their needs seriously. High agent turnover doesn't have to be "the nature of the beast" for your call center.

Empower Agents with the Resources and Authority to Satisfy Customers
by Susan Hash

What call center manager wouldn't want to have a staff of agents who proactively take personal responsibility for the customer's experience? Wishes aside, today it's a necessary element for business success.

Empowering frontline agents by providing them with the knowledge, skills and decision-making authority to take care of callers quickly and efficiently will enable them to represent your company as world class, says JJ Lauderbaugh, president of Lauderbaugh & Associates Inc., a customer relations training and consulting firm in Los Gatos, Calif.

Empowered agents are more committed to the organization's success, she says. "They recognize that they're not just a part of customer service or support, but also involved in marketing and sales."

The nature of the multiple-channel call center environment demands an empowered workforce. The addition of a customer service Web site at HomeSide Lending Inc., a mortgage company headquartered in Jacksonville, Fla., demonstrated that necessity, according to HomeSide Lending's Director of Customer Service Tom Reilly.

Although many of the simpler e-mail responses to customers can be automated, there are also more complex messages that include several inquiries. "Our email customer service agents have to be very skilled and empowered," Reilly says. "They have to have good discernment skills to ensure they're answering all of the customer's questions correctly in the first response."

Initial Obstacles to Overcome

Creating an empowered environment in which agents are focused on customer retention and call center productivity is a journey—and not without a few roadblocks at the start.

Chapter 3

A focus group study of South Florida business leaders by Northwood University revealed that nearly all of the participants said they encountered obstacles in launching empowerment processes. For instance, initially, both managers and staff resisted the effort. Many managers admitted they were reluctant to share decision-making activities with the front line, while others feared losing staff who develop new skills and capacities.

On the frontline side, the study found that staff who seldom had been given a voice in decision making often view the empowerment process with suspicion and distrust. The results further revealed that, at the beginning, organizations suffer a sharp drop in morale and productivity and an increase in turnover among managers and the front line.

Agent Buy-in Is Critical

"Frontline people who have never been given a high degree of responsibility are often afraid of it," says Lauderbaugh. "Or sometimes there's the view that empowerment just means having to do more work."

Probably one of the biggest fears for newly empowered agents is that they will be reprimanded (or worse) for making mistakes.

To get agents to accept decision-making power, Lauderbaugh says it's impor-

---

EMPOWERMENT BARRIERS

A study of employee empowerment in small businesses, conducted by Sam Houston State University, found five common barriers to empowerment:

- A lack of managerial commitment to the concept.
- An unwillingness to change on the part of the employee and/or manager.
- A reluctance on the part of employees to take on responsibility of making decisions.
- Poor communication between employees and managers.
- The failure to realize that, in the short run, performance may dip as empowerment is implemented.

Chapter 3

tant to clearly communicate the specific advantages to the agents of learning new skills and taking on more responsibility.

The ability to advance in their careers is a particularly attractive benefit. At electric appliance manufacturer Braun Inc., the empowerment process offers consumer service reps a visible career growth opportunity. Reps can advance through three tiers to become product specialists, says Consumer Service Manager Ann-Marie O'Keefe. In fact, two of the department's current supervisors were promoted from within, which "is very encouraging for new reps," she says.

Of course, not all agents are the same when it comes to decision-making abilities. "You must know them well enough to understand who is trained and capable of taking responsibility," Lauderbaugh says. Often that has to do with whether or not an individual is goal-oriented. She suggests screening for goal-oriented agents during the recruiting process by asking each candidate what he or she has won in the past. "If someone can't come up with anything that he or she has ever won, they're probably not goal-oriented," she explains. "They haven't given up something to win something."

Different Types of Empowerment

To build an empowered culture, agents need clear decision-making guidelines for dealing with customers. For instance, what's the dollar limit for returns? Can they give away free products? What options can they offer to customers?

Braun consumer service reps have specific policies and procedures for handling different types of product calls. "Our reps are empowered to make decisions, such as whether or not to extend a warranty, provide a repair or a replacement," says O'Keefe. "We don't want callers to have to go to a supervisor for that—it's within the reps' realm of responsibility."

Besides service support, Braun's empowerment process involves product knowledge. The company's 22 consumer service reps are encouraged to learn as much as they can about the various products. (Braun has eight product lines, which include hundreds of appliances and products.) Agents can borrow products to take home and get familiar with them, or they can buy them at a discount.

Through the career progression process, reps can train to be product specialists, and then become responsible for training the rest of the department on their specific products and handling any out-of-the-ordinary calls involving that product.

At HomeSide Lending's Jacksonville call center, agents also increase their level of responsibility as they advance within the center, says Jeanne Babbitt, Jacksonville call center manager. Senior and lead agents are empowered to make more risky decisions than the typical frontline agents. "They provide a support function to the supervisor as well as the phone reps," she says.

Another position in the center is mentor, which is "a very empowered rep who can make supervisory-type decisions and support reps with more complex issues," she says.

Training and Feedback Are Key

A study conducted by Sam Houston State University found training to be an inherent element of empowerment. A well-defined training process ensures "the development of employee skills, as well as the exchange of information about job requirements, organizational performance and customer satisfaction," the study reports.

"Our training and empowerment process starts the minute the rep walks in the door," says HomeSide Lending's Babbitt.

Call center supervisors in her center sit in on new-hire training (which is conducted by corporate training staff) to ensure that it's on target for the call center. "They audit the training content (as well as the response from the class) to make sure it's going to meet our needs once those reps hit the floor in the call center," Babbitt explains. Managers meet with the training staff on a monthly basis to give them feedback on new-hires' progress. "We also provide our training staff with a list of primary call drivers to incorporate into the training to help reps meet customers' needs," she says.

The company's ongoing training process, about 35 hours a year, includes team training, event-driven training (i.e., government regulatory changes, year-end mortgage process changes, etc.) and updates on soft skills.

Continuously Identify Empowerment Opportunities

HomeSide's empowerment process includes a 360-degree review of rep training. Customer service mentors, who support frontline reps, log any calls they receive from reps. The logs are checked regularly to find out how many calls mentors received, from whom and why. Managers can then identify which reps may need additional training, says Tom Reilly. In addition, mentor calls are further dissected to determine any overall training gaps.

The reps themselves can identify empowerment opportunities in focus group sessions that meet on a regular basis or are pulled together for a specific function. "We have focus groups targeted to customer service functions that we handle, such as taxes or insurance. The reps have a very vocal voice in identifying what the empowerment issues are," says Reilly.

In another program, called "Voice of the Customer," reps are encouraged to electronically share caller comments—good or bad—that may be improvement opportunities or simply customer kudos.

Encourage Agent Involvement

Getting agents engaged with other departments helps to foster a sense of commitment to the company. Braun's product specialists act as a liaison between consumer services and marketing. They attend marketing meetings, as well as frequently communicating via e-mail or phone, says O'Keefe.

Product specialists regularly review call data to pinpoint common product issues and offer suggestions to the marketing, quality or technical services departments.

Reps also are encouraged to offer their suggestions for improving processes, such as order turnaround, shipping issues, etc. "The reps are better able to recognize issues quickly because they're the front line," says O'Keefe. "We encour-

Chapter 3

age them not to wait until it shows up on our reports but to constantly share their feedback. Over time, agents become very knowledgeable at all levels. Knowledge is power, and it gives them the ability to handle any issue that comes their way."

Managers Have Responsibilities, Too

Empowerment is not simply a matter of delegating tasks. For call center managers, the leadership responsibilities evolve. "Managers need to be role models to the agents in the call center," says Lauderbaugh.

"They need to focus on growing, mentoring, coaching and counseling their people. As agents witness the empathy supervisors feel for them, as well as concern for their individual growth, they will have a tendency to treat the customers the same way. All call center managers should treat their agents the same as they want their agents to treat callers," she says.

"You have to listen to your employees and your customers," adds Babbitt.

HOW EMPOWERED DO YOUR AGENTS FEEL?

Before beginning an empowerment process, it's important first to assess your call center's needs, as well as your agents' feeling of empowerment with their jobs, says Allen Klose, author of *Breaking the Chains: The Empowerment of Employees—How to Evaluate, Monitor and Improve Employee Empowerment Levels.* Klose suggests conducting a survey that looks at the following areas:

• How empowered do our agents feel?

• Do empowerment levels differ greatly within the department?

• Do our supervisors have different levels of empowerment than our frontline agents?

• Can we develop the specific programs necessary to improve empowerment among our agents?

• If empowerment levels are high, how will this change our strategy of increasing agent involvement?

"Sometimes managers are afraid to give up control but, in the long run, it increases employee satisfaction and customer satisfaction."

Reilly agrees. "That customer satisfaction translates into bottomline savings. One-stop calls are definitely the way to go, and if you empower reps so that they can answer the call and provide a solution that does not result in more calls, then we are dollars and dollars ahead of where we need to be.

"With rep empowerment, you never quite get to the destination because you're always finding new opportunities because of the changing nature of the business that we're in. I encourage my staff not to be satisfied—there's always something more that you can do."

Chapter 3

Low-Cost (and No Cost) Strategies for Retaining Agents

By Beverly Kaye and Sharon Jordan-Evans

One of the toughest challenges contact centers face is agent turnover. Whether the cause is burnout, dissatisfaction with opportunities, the boss or the pay, well-trained people are leaving contact centers faster than they can be replaced.

Despite the recent softening of the job market, good contact center agents are still hard to get and harder to retain. And as the economy improves and employment opportunities increase in other fields, contact centers can be expected to face even greater retention challenges.

Consider the cost of this talent loss. There is no doubt that losing a well-trained contact center agent is expensive. Industry studies indicate that it costs an average of $15,000 to replace a contact center agent. That figure doesn't include the loss of productivity and other costs that are incurred following a talented person's departure and that last throughout the orientation and training of his or her replacement.

Inexpensive New-Hire Retention Strategies

Given the expensive price tag of unwanted turnover, most managers want to do what they can to keep their best people for as long as they possibly can. The good news is, there are many no-cost or low-cost strategies that managers can use to engage and retain talent. These approaches have consistently worked in contact centers across industries—and sometimes despite difficult jobs (with challenging customers) and less than ideal compensation packages. Of course, we're not saying pay doesn't matter. In fact, it is important that you pay agents competitive and fair salaries.

But our research tells us that, beyond pay, there are many other reasons people stay with an organization. Focus on the following strategies and you'll

Chapter 3

63

increase the odds of keeping your best agents and supervisors.

• **Managers (from the top down) must be retention-focused.** A key staff engagement and retention driver often involves developing a new managerial mindset (for some managers and executives). Company leaders must believe that their people are their most critical assets, and that they, as leaders, have more power and influence than anyone else in the retention equation. One company lived this concept particularly well by making employee retention "part of the company DNA." The organization held to that belief by making managers at all levels accountable for engaging and retaining talent.

• **Make sure hiring processes are designed to identify the right agents.** If you hire the right person for the job in the first place, you'll increase your chances of keeping him or her. This means identifying the critical factors that spell success for the job, such as skills, motivations, attitudes, even work style. Many managers interview their top-performing veteran agents to create a baseline. You can then develop interview questions that will reveal whether a candidate does or does not possess those attributes.

During the interview, it's important to ensure that the questions are posed by several people who represent varying management levels and responsibilities. This will ensure that you get different perspectives and input on each candidate.

Regardless of the tough employment market, it's critical to have the courage to reject applicants who, by all indications, won't make it in the long run (even if they're desperately needed in the short run).

• **Develop an effective orientation and welcome process.** The risk for losing call center talent is highest during the first six months of employment. Recognizing that, once they're hired, you'll want to do what you can to "extend the handshake."

An effective method is to develop a solid orientation process with the call center manager in charge of the proceedings—it's not HR's job. The focus must be more involved than simply informing employees where the supplies and break rooms are located. Instead, this is the time for managers to begin developing a meaningful relationship with each new agent.

During orientation, managers should highlight potential career paths (within the contact center and companywide), as well as all learning and enrichment possibilities that are available. The goal is to help each carefully selected new team member to quickly get connected and to visualize his or her future in the organization.

Retaining and Engaging Veteran Agents

What about the agents who are already on the job? How do you retain and engage them? Over the past three years, our two organizations have surveyed more than 14,000 employees from a cross-section of industries about what keeps them on the job. Following are a few instructive findings from our "What Keeps You?" survey.

• **Retention drivers are under the manager's control.** The top five reasons employees stayed with an organization are (in descending order of frequency):

- Exciting and challenging work
- Career growth and development
- Working with great people
- Fair pay
- Good bosses

Yes, pay is on the list. Although many managers believe it is the most important "stay factor" of all, research (ours and many other industry studies) reveals that money consistently falls below other retention drivers. In fact, for decades, researchers have described money as a "hygiene" factor when it comes to employee retention—and it's a dissatisfier when viewed as insufficient, non-competitive or unfair.

But competitive pay will not retain skilled agents if they're bored, see no career path, dislike their colleagues or dislike their bosses. Significantly, four of the top five "stay" factors just mentioned can be influenced by the manager. In fact, most retention drivers are under the manager's control. One survey found that 50 percent of job satisfaction depends on the employee's relationship with the manager. It is because of this incredible influence that organizations are

Chapter 3

increasingly holding managers accountable for hiring, developing, engaging and, yes, retaining talent—even tying managerial compensation and bonuses to retention success.

• **Make the job more interesting.** When the thrill is gone, so are your skilled agents. Job enrichment—making the work more interesting, fulfilling and/or challenging—is a critical retention strategy. It can help you to retain agents, not just physically, but mentally and emotionally, as well. Even if they're physically at their workstations, when agents get bored with the job, they can leave mentally, or "disengage." This surfaces through counterproductive activities, such as high absenteeism and mediocre performance.

Managers, however, can offer various job enrichment opportunities that can help to prevent physical departure and/or disengagement.

Enrichment strategies often take the form of tasks and responsibilities agents can take on in ways that promote personal autonomy and creativity. Or managers might consider offering veteran agents extended training or cross-training opportunities, or a rotation of work assignments to increase job variety. Other possibilities include agent participation in project management, brainstorming sessions to focus on how jobs can be enriched, or agent input on team and/or individual rewards and recognition.

• **Give agents career growth and development opportunities.** Many contact centers are developing career paths for their people, and are getting creative in considering multiple career options (sometimes "upward" positions are in short supply). It's critical for the manager to be involved in this process—agents want their managers to partner with them in discovering and pursuing opportunities at work.

Managers, in turn, need to consider questions like: What's available and what do people want? Would a lateral move be useful or interesting? How can the agent's career goals and the organizational goals and plans mesh? And how can an employee's career goals be accomplished within the context of the contact center structure?

• **People don't leave companies, they leave managers.** Therefore, it's important to show interest and become adept at holding "career conversations" on a regular basis with each agent you hope to keep. These conversations are critical to your agents' development as well as to their sense of belonging and importance to their manager and organization. Regularly touching base with your agents this way will keep them from looking around for greener pastures—and for a boss who cares.

• **Develop a sense of camaraderie among staff.** The third key reason for staying in a job from our "What Keeps You?" survey is the ability to work with great people. Coworker relationships are critical to job satisfaction—and managers who can create a team that works well together and vigorously supports each other are well on the way to building a retention culture.

But doing so requires your time and effort. Successful managers take the time to listen carefully to the needs of each individual, and do what they can to help that person feel fulfilled and satisfied in the job. They also create an atmosphere in which people's needs, opinions, values, work-styles and accomplishments are respected, valued and rewarded. The contact center environment presents some special issues when it comes to work/life balance and the importance of schedule adherence. Savvy managers will recognize their employees' needs and creatively partner with them to find solutions that work. That kind of caring will engender loyalty in a era when many think loyalty is dead.

The Rewards Are Worth the Effort

The tremendous need for more contact centers, coupled with a tight employee market, means that managers need to hire skillfully, and then help their talented agents to grow, develop, and flourish within the contact center environment.

It's a tall order. But it's one that retention-focused contact center managers can efficiently and cost-effectively fill to perfection.

Chapter 3

Enhance Agent Retention by Turning Them Loose
by Greg Levin

If you love somebody, set them free. If you value your agents, do the same. There may be no better way to enhance employee motivation and retention in your call center.

Freeing agents to become actively involved in important nonphone-related programs and projects enables them to show what they can really do, and turns a potentially numbing job into a highly compelling one. The agent position takes on a higher profile—featuring increased prestige, visibility and task variety.

But it's not only about satisfying staff and raising retention rates. "Letting agents loose" on offline projects paves the way for vast improvements in call center processes and overall performance. Collectively, your agents possess a tremendous amount of job and customer knowledge, as well as a wide range of skills and creative abilities. Enabling agents to use that knowledge and expertise to enhance such crucial areas as hiring, training, motivation, quality assurance and interdepartmental relations can make the difference between a mediocre operation and a thriving customer contact center.

Ideas for Agent Emancipation

Here are suggestions on how to expand agent roles to help them and the call center continually evolve and improve:

• **Create agent-led task forces.** Agents respond in big ways when they are given some control over issues that directly affect them in their jobs. Letting them lead special task forces that focus on improvements to key processes— monitoring, scheduling, call center design, etc.—is the best way to turn problem-finders into problem-solvers, says Laura Sikorski, managing partner of consulting firm Sikorski-Tuerpe & Associates in Centerport, N.Y.

"Use the task-force approach for selecting 'complaining agents' to solve an issue," she says. "If an agent doesn't like the current monitoring process, ask him or her to find better ways to evaluate calls. Or create a general task force in charge of creating ways to make agents' jobs easier and more fun. If you give agents the opportunity to change the system, you will be amazed at how motivated and committed they will become."

We can look to Air Canada for a perfect example of the power of agent-led project teams. A few years ago, the airline's Vancouver center was struggling to create and sustain high levels of staff motivation. As a result, the manager, Butch Gregoire, decided to put members of the frontline staff in charge of incentives.

"A team of agents now plans and administers all of our contests and incentives in the call center," explains Gregoire. "We felt it would bring accountability to the staff and add more fun for the agents if their own peers were involved in the coordination of our motivational efforts. Agents have their fingers on the pulse of our center, so they are the natural people to create incentives for everyone." Since introducing the agent-run incentive team, the center has witnessed a dramatic increase in agent enthusiasm and contest participation, as well as improved goal achievement.

- **Implement a formal mentoring program.** Adding a mentoring component—in which veteran staff are paired with new-hires—to your initial training program is a great way to enhance learning and enrich the job for your top agents. A good mentoring program not only raises the comfort level of trainees and ensures that they develop good customer contact habits, it helps to foster cohesive bonds among agents that enhance overall morale in the center.

Mentoring benefits all involved—the mentor, the protégé and the organization as a whole, says Dr. Jan Northup Kratochwill, president of Management Training Systems Inc., a consulting firm specializing in customized training and "mentoring for success" programs. "The mentor gets power, prestige and visibility; the protégé gets confidence; and the organization gets cost-effective training and increased productivity."

Many call centers have already discovered the advantages of mentoring. Since implementing its "New Employee Partners" program—in which trainees partner with experienced agents for nearly a month before "flying solo"—Today's Merchandising call center in Peoria, Ill., has seen a significant increase in overall performance and agent retention.

- **Add peer evaluation to the monitoring mix.** Change the perception of monitoring as a "supervisor vs. staff" battle in your call center by making agents an integral part of your quality assurance team. Call centers that supplement supervisor-led monitoring programs with peer-observation and evaluation often see a noticeable improvement in agent commitment to the center's quality efforts.

"We get the ball rolling and agents take it. They're becoming leaders of the [monitoring program] and doing a great job," says Mimi Steinhorst, supervisor at Lands' End's call center in Cross Plains, Wis., which has used peer monitoring for years. Steinhorst adds that the program has enhanced quality in the call center, as well as agents' communication and coaching skills.

Supervisors benefit from a well-implemented peer monitoring venture, too. Since agents no longer view them as "the enemy," the supervisor-staff bond is strengthened, thus paving the way for higher levels of collaboration and performance improvement.

- **Get agents involved in the hiring process.** Consider creating an agent-led hiring team to help enhance your center's recruiting and selection practices. Ask members to write a detailed job description and an "ideal agent" profile. Have them interview job candidates (after the candidate has interviewed with a manager/supervisor), and take them on a tour of the call center. Later, give members of the hiring team the opportunity to convene as a group to evaluate each candidate and present their selections to supervisors.

Tip: Be sure to rotate existing agents in and out of the hiring team every few months or so to ensure that your entire staff gets the chance to participate.

The benefits of agent-led hiring teams are big. A study conducted by training and consulting firm Response Design Corp. revealed that, when call centers involve agents in the hiring process, "new-hires are better matched with the company culture, begin the job with a clearer understanding of their roles and

Chapter 3

form stronger bonds with coworkers."

• **Tap individual agents' talents.** The opportunities to allow agents to use their unique experiences and capabilities are endless. For example, offer agents who have strong writing skills the opportunity to contribute articles—even a monthly column—to the company newsletter. Let the artists among your staff create posters or other visual aids for special events/contests in the call center. And if you have an agent with outstanding organizational and speaking skills, give him or her the chance to make occasional presentations at call center or interdepartmental meetings.

The benefits of letting agents use their creative talents are priceless, says Tracy Laycock, general manager of Phone Pro, a call center consulting firm specializing in agent training. "Find out what interests them and put them to work... The agent's job satisfaction will increase, customers will be happier and the manager will spend less time conducting interviews due to high turnover."

• **Create "specialist" positions.** Over time, experienced agents become experts on specific products and services, or in specific skills such as cross-selling or dealing with irate customers. Reward these agents by making them a centerwide "specialist" in their area(s) of expertise. Let specialists lead training modules, and encourage other staff members to arrange tutorials with them to improve performance.

In addition to sharing knowledge with fellow agents via coaching and training sessions, product specialists at electric appliance manufacturer Braun Inc. serve as liaisons between the call center and other departments. These agents review call data regarding their specific product(s) and meet with members of marketing, quality or technical services departments to make relevant suggestions. During these meetings, specialists also learn valuable information that can help to improve product training, as well as sales and customer service.

Creating specialist positions also expands the call center career path. Let agents know that becoming a specialist is a key step in the direction of team leader or supervisor—one that brings high visibility, task diversity and a pay increase. Be sure that a formal training and development program is in place to help agents attain "specialist" status.

- **Immerse agents in the enterprise.** The more your entire staff knows about the inner workings of each department, the better they can serve customers and the more clearly they will see how the call center fits into the enterprisewide picture.

As part of initial and ongoing training, send agents on tours of marketing, sales, IT, finance, shipping—and any other departments that interact with the call center directly or indirectly. Encourage agents to conduct informational interviews with managers or supervisors from other areas to further enhance their knowledge.

Don't limit agents' tours to the corporate offices. Let them visit other key sites within the company—i.e., retail stores, bank branches, hotels, restaurants, etc.—to help them see things from the customer's perspective. You may even consider having agents take tours of manufacturing sites. At Arrowhead Water's call center in Brea, Calif., agents visit the company's bottling plants to help them better understand the ins-and-outs of the products they sell and service on the phones every day. Such visits are part of "the full gamut of experience" that agents need to be successful in the call center, says Robin Lyons, manager of employee development.

Set Them Free, Why Don't You?

Merely telling agents that they are highly valued employees who play an important role isn't enough to raise retention and performance. Agents need to see and feel how valued they are and the importance of what they do.

Set agents free on occasion to let them spread their skills and knowledge throughout the call center and enterprise. Otherwise, they'll look to spread those skills and that knowledge someplace else.

Chapter 3

Getting Aggressive with Agent Retention
by Jennifer A. Wilber

High agent turnover is a big problem at most call centers. Unfortunately, the problem is often chalked up to the "nature of the call center beast" by even the most well-intentioned call center professionals. This defeatist attitude is unfortunate, considering the effort and cost involved in hiring and training agents in the first place.

Dramatically reducing turnover doesn't have to be an overwhelming task. There are many actions call center managers can take every day to get aggressive with agent retention. The success of every inbound call center depends on experienced, high quality frontline staff, thus the last thing managers should want to see is any of those quality agents walking out the door.

Agent retention is affected by a number of factors over which call center managers can exercise ample control. This article summarizes what every manager can do to ensure that their valued agents stick around and serve customers well for as long as possible.

Develop Tigers during Training

A successful agent retention strategy begins on the first day of training. Remind trainees of the crucial role that agents play in the call center, of their intrinsic value to the organization. Inspire new-hires to perform right from the start.

During initial training, provide key background information on the call center, the company and its customers. Describe the agent's job in detail, including the exciting opportunities that lie ahead. The training program itself needs to not only cover the knowledge and skill sets agents need to succeed, but also to incorporate creative games and interactive exercises to help enhance learning and break up the monotony of the passive classroom setting.

Provide ample training time to enable trainees to effectively learn all aspects of handling calls for your company. Measure their performance regularly and

Chapter 3

provide constant positive feedback. New agents often resign because they are thrown on the phones before they've grasped the key aspects taught during training. These agents don't quit because they are lazy, rather they often lack confidence due to insufficient training practices. It is essential for managers to ensure that agents know how to effectively handle calls before agents begin talking to customers on the phones.

Maintain Consistency, Manage Proactively

Another key retention factor is to maintain consistency by having policies and procedures in place that every manager and supervisor follows. Agents become unhappy with their jobs and mistrustful of their manager/supervisors if they perceive that some agents receive preferential treatment. Ensure that formal, yet realistic guidelines exist surrounding such key call center issues as attendance, adherence to schedule, and call monitoring, and that these guidelines are fully understood by both agents and managers/supervisors. Inconsistent policies and/or subjective treatment invariably lead to high agent turnover in the call center.

Proactive management is also essential for improving agent retention. Managers who act only after major problems occur will constantly find themselves "behind the eight ball," resulting in hasty decisions and poor treatment of agents. Proactive call center managers take a more holistic and preventive approach—focusing on continual agent development and learning to avoid major performance problems.

Proactive managers incorporate two key practices into their management methods: 1) They actively coach and monitor all agents throughout their employment. Managers who actively search for ways to enhance agents' value and make them more successful will certainly reduce turnover. 2) Proactive managers serve as role models for staff. They are honest, energetic, accessible, and dedicated to enhancing customer satisfaction. Every action you as a call center manager take affects how agents perceive their job and their value. Managers who are courteous and patient will inspire agents to be friendly to customers

Chapter 3

and to take time to help them with complex transactions/problems. If managers act tired, bored or frustrated, agents will likely feel the same way, treat customers poorly and soon seek alternative employment.

Attack Retention by Customizing Agent Support

To be truly effective in battling agent attrition, call center managers need to consider the length of time that each agent has worked in the center and provide the appropriate type of support. Managers should be aware of the specific needs of three categories of frontline employees: 1) graduated trainees, 2) new agents, and 3) veterans. This will enable managers to attack the retention problem head on and develop a team of quality agents who will stay on board for years to come.

Let's take a closer look at each employee category and the appropriate actions you can take to foster confidence, enthusiasm and a sense of empowerment.

1. Graduated Trainees: Graduated trainees are the people fresh out of training and on the phones. All managers and supervisors—not just the person who conducted the initial training classes—need to pay special attention to these employees. Keep in mind how the first day feels working in a fast-moving, dynamic call center environment. Make sure these employees feel comfortable and are excited about being part of the agent team. Shower them with enthusiasm. Here are some specific tips:

- Take time to welcome them personally.
- Learn and use the graduated trainees' names whenever you speak with them.
- Give them a detailed tour of the call center and introduce them to other agents.
- Set achievable, realistic goals for the first day (e.g., taking a call with a smile, becoming more comfortable with call procedures, etc.), and reinforce those goals throughout the day.
- Provide praise and recognition whenever possible.
- Reassure them that they can do the job and that they'll be successful if

Chapter 3

they simply use what they have learned in training.

- Take some extra time to role-play one on one or in small groups if any graduated trainees are having difficulties.

- Conduct an upbeat wrap-up meeting. Talk with each agent individually at the end of their first shift and encourage them to ask questions. Review goals for the day and training topics.

2. New Agents: The employees in this category include agents who have been on the phones in the call center for anywhere from a week to a month or two. Very few people are "naturals" at a job; it takes time to learn the ropes and excel. New agents are often forgotten about whenever an even newer group of trainees graduate and hit the phones. Here are some suggestions to keep new agents from feeling abandoned:

- Sit down and talk with them informally, and use their names.

- Compliment any improvement since their first day, week, etc.

- Check in with them often and ask how things are going so far.

- Set achievable, realistic and increasingly challenging goals for the near future.

- Include those who have been there for a month or more in recognition opportunities and contests (e.g., provide certificates for "most improved agent," "friendliest agent," etc.).

- Recognize "mini-anniversaries," such as "happy first week" or "happy first month." Ideally, this should be done in front of other agents at shift changes, staff meetings, etc.

3. Veterans: These are the agents who have been with you for several months or years. While many of these agents perform very well, some may begin using incorrect behaviors as their performance goes relatively unchecked by managers/supervisors. Therefore, they must receive ample support and feedback. It is important to do everything possible to make them feel appreciated for their longevity, as they can be excellent role models for new employees. Here's some advice that works:

- Recognize their good performance regularly with tangible or intangible rewards.

- Involve them in agent training. This can include having them serve as model agents for trainees to "shadow" for a day or two, or asking them to give brief presentations in training classes on how to effectively handle certain calls. You may even consider letting your star agents help with the design of your training program.
- Meet with these employees to discuss career/skill path opportunities and possible timelines.
- Ask them for suggestions for contest ideas, incentives, etc.
- Assess their performance regularly and provide salary increases when appropriate.
- Set challenging goals for them with incentives.
- Acknowledge anniversaries of veterans ("happy six months," "one year," etc). Include a small reward such as time off or gift certificates.

Not a Futile Endeavor

Enhancing agent retention is not a futile endeavor. Dramatic improvements can easily be made by paying close attention to agents' specific needs and learning styles, and by constantly reminding them of their value to the organization. Proactive call center managers who provide thorough training, maintain consistency, foster enthusiasm and treat agents as valuable individuals rather than merely the "people on the phones" will retain high-quality employees and ensure the call center's overall success for years to come.

Chapter 3

A Decade of Service the Average for Agents at MedicAlert Call Center

by Julia Mayben

Ask MedicAlert's 56 phone agents what they were doing 10 years ago, and chances are they'll respond, "The same as today." Unlike most call centers that struggle with chronic agent turnover, MedicAlert's center, located in Turlock, Calif., has a virtually non-existent attrition rate.

The average agent tenure at MedicAlert is 10 years. One agent has been with the center for more than 21 years. Keeping staff in place hasn't been a difficult task, says Laura Biewer, operations manager for MedicAlert, a 41-year-old non-profit organization that offers medical information and identification services to its members.

"Our agents stay because the work is meaningful to them," Biewer explains. "It's not that management has to do anything special. The agents feel a connection with the work they do and a loyalty to the MedicAlert members." Biewer could be accused of downplaying the role that management plays in keeping agents situated, as she and her colleagues take hiring and training very seriously and have ample reward and recognition programs in place.

What makes the agents' commitment even more impressive is the fact that they work in an often-stressful environment that is supported by little modern technology. The center's basic ACD sends agents more than a half-million calls a year—about 20,000 are emergency calls in which how the agent responds can determine life or death.

The importance of the calls motivates rather than intimidates the MedicAlert staff.

"It's the service we provide—helping people in need—that keeps me coming back day after day," says Louise Onate, an agent of 11 years. "You get to know the members and realize they depend on you."

Chapter 3

Responding in Times of Crisis

Biewer agrees that handling emergency calls is the primary reason the 24x7 call center exists. Emergency calls come in whenever somebody dials the number located on the back of a pendant or bracelet worn by a MedicAlert member. "These calls support the real purpose of why we are here," says Biewer. "In an emergency, we can provide a caller with information about the emblem-wearer's identity, next of kin, primary physician and medical conditions." All emergency calls take priority and are answered on the first ring. When these calls come in, a bell is heard throughout the center to alert agents to the nature of the call. Any agent can answer an emergency call, thus ensuring that it is handled immediately.

In between handling the adrenaline-pumping emergency calls, agents take non-emergency calls from prospective and existing members. As Biewer explains, "People who are not MedicAlert members can contact us on our toll-free number for information about our services. We also take calls from existing members who want to update the information we keep on file for them, or to order a new MedicAlert emblem." In addition, the center occasionally receives calls from people who want to give a donation.

While such calls don't have the immediate life-or-death impact the emergency calls can have, they are taken just as seriously. "We stress to agents that all the calls they handle relate to our mission here: to protect and save lives," Biewer says. "If they don't do a good job handling the non-emergency calls, like when they interview a member for medical information, then we're not going to have a good record to relay later in an emergency."

That message comes through loud and clear to agents. "It's not like we're taking orders for shirts," says agent Onate. "A member's well-being—even their life—may be dependent on the information we're putting into the computer."

Agents' dedication to doing a good job is evidenced by the center's performance, which includes a long-standing track record of meeting and exceeding service level targets. For example, the center has consistently answered 80 percent of calls in 26 seconds in recent months, surpassing its established tar-

Chapter 3

get of 80/30. Abandonment has remained less than 3 percent.

Hiring and Training for Longevity

The center's careful hiring and training practices have helped to secure agent longevity. All agents must have at least one year of experience in a medical environment and be familiar with medical terms. Most agents have worked in a doctor's office or a hospital, or for a health insurance company dealing with medical claims. A few are certified nurse assistants.

MedicAlert's hiring process includes phone interviews, conducted by Biewer, to test applicants' voice skills and customer service potential. Those who pass the initial screening are invited to the center to take a test to determine typing and spelling skills, as well as knowledge of medical terminology.

Once hired, agents complete a 12-week intensive training program—led by Biewer and a quality assurance trainer—which focuses on computer and customer service skills, MedicAlert procedures and policies, and an area Biewer calls "Call Center Orientation 101." As she explains, "That's where I review the productivity measurements we use, and how the agents can achieve what we want them to achieve." About 75 percent of the training takes place in a classroom setting. New-hires spend the remaining 25 percent of the time in the call center listening in on calls with an experienced agent.

Trainers place special emphasis on how to handle emergency calls. "Agents are trained to screen callers to determine what the situation is and where they are calling from," says Biewer. "If it's a non-medical person calling, the agent taking the call won't give out specific information, but will offer to stay on the line with them until medical help arrives. If it's a medical professional calling, agents can give medical information. If needed, they will follow up the conversation by faxing a copy of the person's record."

Toward the final weeks of new-hire training, trainees spend time with experienced agents listening in on calls. They are later given mail-order applications to process, which often requires follow-up calls to the members. Throughout training, supervisors audit the work of all new-hires. Once trainers score 90 per-

Chapter 3

cent accuracy on completed work, they begin taking inbound calls.

Registered nurses are on staff at the center to provide ongoing training and coaching for agents when needed. Additionally, agents meet with Biewer in small groups of five to six every two weeks to review medical information and to sharpen customer service skills.

This ongoing training keeps long-term staff fresh. "It seems like we are training all the time, but the agents need reinforcement because we expect them to remember and do so much," says Biewer.

Recognition Keeps Agents Rallying

MedicAlert recognizes agents' good work whenever possible to foster enthusiasm and fend off burnout. For example, they receive a gold ribbon whenever the center gets a letter complimenting their work. Currently, 30 of the 56 agents have received ribbons since the program started. Agents also receive food, such as pizza, bagels and fruit, to keep them charged up on the phones. On occasion, they receive cash bonuses for effectively handling high call volumes.

In addition to these rewards and incentives, agents receive special gifts and participate in fun activities during the center's annual customer service appreciation week. For example, one year, agents were given chocolate telephones one day and access to a mocha bar another day. Each agent also received either a silver bracelet with a telephone charm or a telephone pin.

Biewer also has plans to roll out an incentive plan for staff that will be based on the center's service level, which she believes will help the center move from its current service level goal of 80/30 to a new goal of 80/20. The proposed incentive plan will enables agents to earn a nominal monetary reward each month that service level targets are met, with a larger monetary award given each quarter the goals are regularly achieved.

While the program is still in the planning stage, agents were given a voice in deciding what type of incentive program should be implemented. "We let agents vote on whether they wanted it based on team or individual scores, and they decided it should be an 'all or nothing' team award," says Biewer.

Chapter 3

Dedication Compensates for Lack of Modern Tools

Veteran staff have been able to provide good service for years without the benefits of advanced technology. Non-emergency calls, which come in to the center on a different line than the emergency calls, are routed by the center's Meridian Max ACD. When agents answer these calls, they have no way of knowing what the nature of the call is, other than the fact that it is not an emergency. Once they determine the caller's needs, agents can pull up information on their personal computer.

All calls are answered by a live voice; the center doesn't use a voice response unit. "The only time a caller gets a recording is on a non-emergency line if all lines are busy," Biewer says.

Biewer admits that the center has been slow to add modern call center technology, but sees that changing. In the past, the company didn't invest in call center technology because it didn't see a need. As she explains, "When we had the money, it was invested in computer systems, not on technology to handle calls."

Today the company realizes the importance of the call center in achieving MedicAlert's mission, which has brought about a new interest in call center technology. "We now know that certain tools will help us manage the call center more efficiently and help agents do their jobs better. We've been evaluating what we need and are putting aside capital in preparation of that," says Biewer.

Recently, the center added TCS' workforce management software to help with forecasting and scheduling. Biewer has also been exploring new call monitoring software, which incorporates voice and data, to enable her to record agents' calls for coaching and training purposes.

Even without the new technology, the impressive agent longevity and dedication at MedicAlert isn't likely to change. "The work we do here is a lot more powerful than selling long-distance service," says Biewer. "That's what has kept the agents here doing the best job they can. And that's what will continue to drive them."

Chapter 3

AmFac Parks and Resorts Cuts Agent Turnover with Elaborate Career Path

by Julia Mayben

In its first year of operation, the AmFac Parks and Resorts call center in Denver, Colo., was plagued with staffing problems and, consequently, poor customer service. At the heart of the problem was an agent turnover rate that had soared past the 90-percent mark.

"Agents were getting burned out and leaving," recalls Terry Metzger, director of central reservations for the AmFac Parks and Resorts call center. "We realized that we needed to encourage agents to stay with the company, that we needed to develop something for which they could strive."

Management's solution was to create a formal career path program. The program, which was introduced in late fall of 1996, features different job levels that agents can rise to after receiving extensive training and passing certification and recertification requirements. Employees can move through the ranks from new agent to master agent to lead agent, and ultimately to supervisor. They receive pay increases with each move up the ladder.

Metzger and the agents are seeing the program's benefits. Turnover in the call center has decreased dramatically to less than 30 percent, a level that is well within the hospitality call center average. "Most agents are now looking at their jobs here as a career," Metzger says. Besides the lure of future jobs in the call center, the career path offers agents variety. Says Metzger, "Agents can learn more skills and use those skills to do different jobs than simply answering the phones day after day. That helps keep them from burning out."

The program makes management happy, too. With employee training as a centerpiece of the career path, the center is developing agents who are able to provide better customer service. "More agents are staying with us and getting more training," says Metzger. "With people trained in all functions, we can shift directions quickly if we need to. We're providing a whole different level of service."

The Denver call center, which employs 40 full-time equivalent agents, is the

Chapter 3

largest of three AmFac Parks and Resorts call centers in the United States. The Denver operation handles reservations and information calls for lodges and recreation centers at the Grand Canyon's North and South Rims, Bryce Canyon, Zion Canyon and Death Valley. It is the only AmFac call center to have introduced a formal career path program.

The First Rung

The career path program is introduced to AmFac agents when they are first hired. "We give them a career guide booklet that tells them all about the program, and review the information with them so they know up front what the program is all about and what opportunities are available to them," explains Scott Willey, a training supervisor at the call center.

New-hires can begin climbing the call center career ladder after completing two weeks of training, which is led by supervisors and lead agents, and a 90-day review period where agents begin taking calls. During the initial training and review periods, agents are tested frequently and must receive passing grades before advancing. "New agents must maintain an 85 percent average on tests about products, computer skills and customer service skills when they finish their two-week training," says Willey. During the 90-day review, agents are rated via weekly monitoring of calls, as well as reviews of the confirmation reports that they complete and send to customers who make reservations. "We make sure that they are well-trained and ready for the next level," Willey explains.

Moving to the Master Level

Agents who successfully complete their review are eligible to begin training for the next level, that of master agent. This training averages four to six weeks and can be scheduled at the agent's discretion. Most who opt to train for the master agent position begin within a few months of becoming eligible. "Most of our people take a little breather—sometimes up to six months—before they begin training for the master agent position," says Metzger. "But we do have a few fast-trackers who begin scheduling their training immediately after their successful

90-day review."

The master agent training program covers the various functions in the call center, including processing faxes, handling advance deposits and Internet requests, as well as conducting night audits. "We rotate them through each function," Metzger explains. "One day, they might work on customers' advance deposits; another day, they might work on handling Internet requests. Agents receive training on each function, including one-on-one tutoring, if needed."

After each training session, agents are tested on how well they demonstrate the skills needed for the particular function. Once they have achieved passing grades for each function, they are deemed a certified master agent and receive a pay increase.

But the testing doesn't stop there. Agents must undergo recertification for each function. "How often agents must be recertified in a particular area depends on the complexity of the function," says Metzger. "For example, for things like processing faxes, we do annual recertifications. But for the night audits, which involve uploading reservation information into the computer each night, agents need to be recertified every quarter."

Ongoing agent training also consists of onsite inspections of the parks that the center handles. "We take agents on field trips to the parks so they can see the lodges and experience firsthand the different trails. That gives us experts on the phone who really know the parks," Metzger says.

While the training required to become and remain a master agent may be rigorous, most employees take on the challenge—and succeed. Over half of the staff at the center are certified master agents, according to Metzger. He believes the agents are motivated to climb the career ladder not merely for the pay increase, but for the increased job satisfaction. "The career path is our official way to acknowledge their efforts, reward them, recognize them and give them new challenges," he says.

As a trainer, Willey says the program also appeals to agents because they like being part of a team. "The training gives them a better overall picture of what the call center does. They are enthusiastic because they are part of a team effort

Chapter 3

accomplishing new things and learning new skills."

Ambitious Agents in the "Lead"

Master agent is the highest position for which some staff will strive. "Some want to stay there," says Metzger. "For them, it's a perfect fit."

But for more ambitious agents, the next rung up from master agent is a "lead," a position Metzger says has evolved into a supervisory support position. "When we first opened the call center, the leads were doing many of the functions in the call center, what the master agents are doing today. Leads still take calls when needed, but now, because of the growing number of master agents who are available to take over those tasks, leads now have more time to learn how to manage and motivate people."

Unlike the master agent position, which is open to all agents who pass the certification process, the AmFac call center has only three lead positions—one for each supervisor. When a lead position becomes available, qualified master agents at the center are considered for the opening.

Metzger describes the center's leads as "supervisors in training." Each lead works closely with one supervisor, acting like an apprentice. "The leaders help conduct meetings with agents, do interviews with potential employees and provide coaching for agents," explains Metzger.

Like the master agents, leads receive extensive instruction. Training for leads is conducted by the company's human resources department and covers a wide range of supervisory "how-to's" on employee interviewing, coaching, counseling and personnel reviews. If needed, leads can receive one-on-one training.

Shaping Superior Supervisors

On occasion, a supervisory position, the highest rung on the career ladder, may open up. Only leads are considered for such positions. Candidates are interviewed by the remaining supervisors and Metzger. "We fill the position with the best lead," he says. "We look at things like how long they have been a lead, the work they have done and the progress they have made."

Chapter 3

The supervisor's job is to manage and motivate a call team. This includes everything from holding periodic team meetings to overseeing agents' daily performances and conducting performance evaluations. Supervisors also are responsible for keeping up with new park information. "They need to know details about each location," explains Metzger. "They go to the parks frequently and develop relationships with the supervisors at each park."

Supervisors receive extensive training, though it is more informal than the training that the leads and master agents receive. The company's human resources department conducts the training sessions for supervisors. "We've established training courses on how to coach staff and how to provide positive reviews," says Metzger. Supervisors also attend training sessions—led by training consultants—on issues such as employee motivation and coaching.

Employees Going for Goals, Not the Throat

Metzger is pleased with the level of competition the career path program has spawned among employees. "We're getting better performance from them and they are pushing themselves harder trying to do a good job," he says.

Willey agrees. "It's the positive kind of competition, not the cut-throat variety. I see people going back over their work two or three times just to make sure they are doing it right. They are motivated to do the best job possible and meet the quality goals."

Chapter 3

Chapter 4: Integrate Retention in Recruiting Processes

Forward-thinking organizations focus on "retention" while recruiting and selecting staff for their call centers. These companies take the search for and screening of candidates very seriously—carefully defining job descriptions and testing for core agent attributes and values before bring somebody on board.

How to Develop a Retention-Oriented Agent Recruiting and Selection Process

By Anita O'Hara

Managers in this people-intensive business of customer care are aware that their employee costs generally comprise about 80 percent of a typical operating budget. Did you know that by focusing solely on cutting your attrition by two percentage points per month, you can reduce your operating expenses by almost 10 percent? Not only that, you'll also reap additional benefits, such as improved customer satisfaction through more consistent customer service and higher employee satisfaction.

That sounds like a great payback, doesn't it? And yet, so much easier to say than to do.

So what's the secret? Managers need to work at viewing agent retention from a holistic standpoint. It's not enough to have retention-oriented team leaders on board who regularly incent and recognize agent performance with contests and special events. It's not enough to develop a solid training approach or a rich career path process.

Instead, success is a combination of all of these things, or in other words, in creating a solid retention program from the start—when the agent joins the call center—through every single "moment of truth" that involves the agent.

The "retention wheel" in Figure 1, on the next page, illustrates all of the areas to focus on that are key to creating a solid plan. This article will focus on the first step, recruitment and selection.

There are six fundamental steps in the recruitment and selection process:

1. Analyze job tasks.
2. Identify specific skills and competencies required.
3. Describe the performance required by the job.
4. Develop a job description.
5. Identify source pools and a recruitment plan.
6. Define and implement your selection process.

Chapter 4

Analyzing Job Tasks

The first two steps can be completed concurrently. Begin by taking a detailed look at your top-performing agents. Consider both the efficiency and effectiveness with which they perform their tasks. It may also be useful to re-review your star agents' resumes. In addition, take time to observe and conduct followup interviews with a group of "experts" performing their jobs. Try to identify common tasks they perform well.

Use this analysis to create a list of skills that are critical, such as communication and articulation, analytical skills, organizational skills (talk and type/overlapping), call center or customer service experience, listening skills and computer skills.

If you are creating a customer service organization from the ground up, and have no stars from which to create a standard, try benchmarking with a similar type of company. Generally, you'll find that, regardless of industry, call center managers are looking for agents with similar skills.

FIGURE 1: THE RETENTION WHEEL

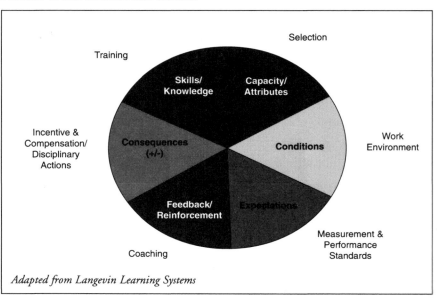

Adapted from Langevin Learning Systems

Next, consider which competencies or behaviors you want your prospective employees to demonstrate. A few common competencies include: positive attitude, flexibility, teamwork and cooperation, customer orientation, self-reliance and stamina. There are a variety of companies that can help you identify these, and which can even create a hiring instrument that will improve your retention rates.

Writing a Job Description Aimed at High Performance

Once you know what type of agent you're looking for, you can identify the type of performance required and write your job description. At this stage, you're prioritizing your desired and required skills and competencies, describing the work environment in which employees will coexist, identifying the scope and breadth of the job (e.g., what kinds of decisions will prospective agents make?).

In addition, this is the point at which you should identify the agents' pay structure. It's best to include two key groups in this process:

• Human resources can help to assess compensation in the external market. They can also help to price your jobs comparable to other jobs within the organization.

• The senior leadership team can help you to identify your pay strategy. That is, do you want to be the employer of choice or simply pay the market average?

Finding Staff Sources

Every staff selection strategy should include recruitment sources as well as a selection plan. It's important to track your sources and analyze their success over time. For each candidate hired, be sure to track and record the following: 1) source; 2) performance; 3) attendance record; and 4) tenure.

In this manner, you can determine the success of each source. If one source yields consistently high-performing agents who stay, keep using it. If, on the other hand, a source results in an agent pool that regularly turns over, it's time to stop recruiting through that source. The following are a few common recruit-

Chapter 4

ment sources:

- Employee referrals—from the top-performing agents who fit well into your work environment.

- Advertising—in local newspapers or trade publications.

- College recruitment—works best with part-time staff, preferably with a good tuition reimbursement program as a benefit.

- Physically challenged—check to see if there is a state program that will work with your center to assess the environment and help to curtail the costs of special equipment.

- Career fairs by invitation—be sure to publicize it widely. Have candidates send resumes in advance. Call prescreened candidates to invite them (or not) to your event. Be sure to set up interview rooms in advance for interviews and/or role-play exercises.

- Internet—candidates who browse recruiting Web sites are likely to be Internet-savvy.

Defining and Implementing a Selection Process

The last step is to define and implement your selection process. There are a variety of tools that you can employ in this process.

It's important to carefully consider the sequence of these events. For instance, Figure 2, on the next page, illustrates a sample process.

The most common pitfall managers make during the final selection is to put too much weight on a single facet of the screening/interview process. For instance, a candidate may be terrified by the job interview, yet have an excellent background, great references, score well on the behavioral screen, and present himself in an excellent fashion during the phone screen. Consider all parts of the process, as well as the weight you will attach to each, before making your final selection.

As you can see, a lot of work goes into an effective agent recruitment and selection process—from brainstorming and describing your ideal call center agent all the way to the sequence and timing of the final selection process. But if you take the time to plan your strategy well, it will start with selecting a star performer and end with retaining one!

FIGURE 2: CUSTOMER SERVICES SELECTION CYCLE

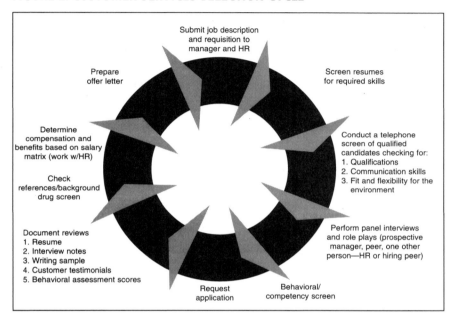

Cut Agent Turnover by Hiring for Motivational Fit

by Michelle Cline

Do you have an agent in your call center who has the experience, knowledge and skills for the job, but who still performs below his or her potential? What about an agent who has the right skills, but is frequently tardy or absent? Have you ever hired someone who just didn't fit with your corporate culture? Just about every manager can answer "yes" to at least one of these questions.

The harder question to answer is "Why?" How can an employee possess the right skills for the job, yet not succeed? An elusive, yet key, recruiting component is motivational fit—understanding whether or not the candidate's motivation matches your call center's needs.

Screening resumes, conducting traditional interviews and other typical assessment tools have limited success in consistently and accurately pinpointing a candidate's skills and abilities that pertain to the job. However, attempting to measure motivation and attitude accurately with these methods is even more difficult.

Determining a candidate's fit for the job with traditional interviews, general personality tests or references is as accurate as flipping a coin. So how do you accurately determine a candidate's skills, abilities and, importantly, motivation to do the job?

Developing a hiring system that accurately measures job success factors, especially motivation and attitude, is the key to hiring the right people—the top performers—for your call center.

Understanding Your Needs

To know exactly whom you should hire, you must first understand the skills, attitudes, interests and motivations that make an agent successful in your call center. This involves much more than just writing a job description with job requirements. It includes understanding the type of work that is done, the skills

Chapter 4

and motivations it takes to complete this work, the expectations that are set for agents, and the cultural aspects of the company that are critical for success.

While analyzing the call center agent job for your organization, you should concentrate on compiling a group of "success factors" that can be used to create a "success profile." This profile will be your starting point for understanding the competencies required for an agent to be successful in your center.

Officially, this process is known as conducting a job analysis. It's defined by the Department of Labor as: "A detailed statement of work behaviors and other information relevant to the job." Conducting a job analysis allows you to identify your call center's success profile, as well as provides you with the legal documentation you need to support your hiring practices.

Types of Success Factors

Typically, there are four types of success factors for the call center environment. These fall into one of the following categories:

1. Cognitive ability
2. Planning and organizing
3. Interpersonal
4. Attitudes, interests and motivations

The major difference between these categories is "can do" vs. "will do." Cognitive ability, planning and organizing, and interpersonal categories are

---

CALL CENTER SUCCESS FACTORS

Cognitive ability (can do)
Apply information = productivity
Examples: problem-solving, learning and applying information.

Planning (can do)
Organizing ability = efficiency
Examples: planning ability, organizing ability, adherence to policies, following rules, accuracy.

Interpersonal (can do)
Persuasion = upselling
Examples: customer service, persuasion, getting along with others, teamwork, coaching ability.

Motivation (will do)
Attitude toward work = turnover
Examples: Attitude toward work, attendance, flexibility, going above and beyond, energy.

Chapter 4

"can do's." In other words, can a candidate do what you need him or her to do? Attitudes, interests and motivations are the elusive "will do's." This category looks at: "Will the candidate do what is required of him or her?" This is one of the most challenging and critical areas to measure.

Selecting the Right Candidate

Once you have identified the success factors, you must then answer the question: "How am I going to determine if my candidate possesses these factors?" According to the Department of Labor guidelines, a multiple-hurdle hiring approach is most effective in making an accurate hiring decision.

A successful multiple-hurdle hiring approach should allow you to assess all needed success factors using lower cost tools in the beginning of the recruiting process, and saving higher cost methods until after you've narrowed your applicant pool.

Typically, most job interviews focus on skills. For example: "Does the candidate possess the problem-solving skills necessary to do the job?" However, this type of interviewing neglects the "will do" part of the job. By assessing motivations, you can determine whether or not the candidate *wants* to use their problem-solving skills in your center.

Evaluating candidates for motivational fit can be challenging. You can use one of the many assessment tools available on the market to help you gauge whether or not a candidate's motivations pertain to job performance. These tools are generally computer- or Web-based, or can be administered via pencil and paper. Most can provide you with results that indicate how closely the candidate's "motivational fit" matches your call center's needs.

To follow up the motivational assessment, you may also choose to conduct a structured behavioral interview to pinpoint weak areas of motivation. For instance, if the candidate's results indicated that he or she might not have enough flexibility for your organization, you can ask questions that focus on flexibility. After you have heard the candidate's responses, you can make a more informed hiring decision.

Chapter 4

Combining motivational fit assessments with behavioral-based interviews is a thorough way to measure attitudes, interest and motivations for the job. Selecting candidates based on both their skills and motivations will help you to decrease turnover. And an additional benefit: You'll have a staff of agents who enjoy coming to work in your call center.

Chapter 4

Call Center Spotlight: Budco
by Julia Mayben

Like most call centers, Budco has experienced its share of agent turnover. Recently, though, taking a cue from its corporate initiative of "attracting outstanding lifelong employees," management beefed up the call center hiring and retention program—with big results.

Budco is a marketing services firm located in Highland Park, Mich. that handles inbound and outbound sales and customer service needs related to ongoing client programs. "In our environment, reducing turnover is particularly important because we have over 80 different programs going on at any time and we cross-utilize resources where we can. To lose someone after investing a great deal of training time hurts us," explains Janet Smith, director of customer support services, who along with Joy Labadie, vice president of customer support, spearheaded the revamped hiring and retention program.

Start with the Right People

The initiative begins with hiring, which Smith says is the heart of the program. It's a three-part process that involves an initial telephone interview to assess verbal skills, a written test for spelling and grammar skills, and a personal interview at the center to determine if a candidate is a good match for the Budco culture.

Previously, the company's human resources department handled some of the hiring duties, but now the call center's management staff handle the entire process. "Human resources can do basic screening but, when it comes down to the details and competencies, we know the answers we're looking for. I believe it's better supported from our perspective," Labadie says.

The hiring responsibility adds to the workload, but she says the investment is worth it in the long run. "You can put in the time upfront or spend twice as much time at the back end."

Chapter 4

Engage New Agents

The next step in the program focuses on "engagement"—making new agents quickly feel like a part of the team. Agents are encouraged to take ownership in specific areas, such as developing awards and incentives for the center. Additionally, management encourages two-way communication. For example, they coordinate frequent small team meetings as well as center-wide town hall meetings on Saturdays that allow management and agents to address issues in-depth.

Perhaps just as important is agent participation in determining their work schedules. "We provide the staff with our phone requirements, such as the number of agents we need and when," says Smith. "We don't care what the schedule looks like as long as we're meeting the customers' demands. It's a great way for agents to take ownership—it gives them a sense of control."

While that process may sound complicated, it isn't tough to manage, says Smith. "We have many different small groups, which allows us to offer more flexibility to agents."

> **BUDCO AT-A-GLANCE**
>
> **Location:** Highland Park, Colo.
>
> **Hours of operation:** 8 a.m. until midnight, Monday through Friday
>
> **FTEs:** 175 (250 during peak season)
>
> **Services provided:** Customer service, sales support
>
> **Channels handled:** Primarily phone
>
> **Notable:** Initiated a hiring/training program that lowered turnover and training costs, while increasing productivity and morale

Growth Opportunities Build Leaders

The final step in the hiring and retention program targets leadership, coaching and development. In addition to the initial orientation and computer training all new-hires receive, there is in-depth product training, which typically lasts between one and four weeks. The focus during training is on fun and creativity. For instance, agents assigned to merchandising programs are required to have first-hand experience of the merchandise. They'll often put on "fashion shows" to educate others on the team about the products.

To keep agents motivated about their work, career paths are charted for those who have long-term ambitions within the center or company. And for those who aren't interested in climbing the career ladder, managers ensure they get a lot of diversity in their work through various projects and programs.

Happier Agents Translates into Lower Costs

Since implementing the comprehensive program, the call center has experienced productivity gains in several areas, including a significant decrease in call-handle times. But there have been other impressive benefits, including a considerable drop in staff turnover. And because fewer new people need to be trained, the center has cut its training costs in half.

What's more, agent morale has improved. According to Smith, agents have positive comments about the new environment. "I've had people say that it's a totally different environment here; that they're getting to know the people they're working with. There's no revolving door any more."

Chapter 4

Chapter 5: Eliminate Job Frustrations

There are plenty of things about typical call center work and design that drive agents crazy—but nobody said that your call center had to be typical. Top centers do a great job of identifying and removing the common obstacles to agent performance and morale, as well as determining the tools, policies and processes that need to be added to ensure high employee satisfaction and commitment.

The fast-paced, high-volume environment leads to excessive agent attrition in many call centers. However, effective practices and programs to reduce stress can increase enthusiasm and stop the staff exodus.

Agent stress can be dramatically reduced via proven practices, such as compelling recognition and development programs, empowering staff to participate in decisions that affect their jobs, training supervisors to be "emotional coaches," and ensuring that performance objectives are fair and feasible.

Battling Agent Burnout
by Greg Levin

Average turnover rates ranging from 30 to 50 percent. Problems with employee absenteeism and adherence to schedule. An increase in the number of agents seeking union representation. These are the symptoms of a highly disgruntled call center workforce.

But what is the cause? The answer according to many is, frighteningly, the inherent nature of the call center environment itself. The call center is, by no fault of management or anybody else, a place where agents must stay seated alone for hours while efficiently handling high volumes of often-repetitive contacts from increasingly demanding customers.

Isn't it only natural that the people working day after day in this kind of atmosphere soon become tired and disenfranchised?

Yes—*if* the leaders in the call center don't do anything to *battle* the burnout. According to a study of call center workers by the Australian Services Union, "unsupportive" managers are one of the most common factors leading to stress in the call center. Agent respondents pointed specifically to a lack of communication and encouragement from managers—as well as a need for more training and opportunities within the call center—as key sources of early burnout.

Numerous other call center studies report similar findings.

However, this is not to suggest that all call centers are plagued with unsupportive leaders and aggravated agents. The fact is, many progressive managers have implemented a variety of practices to help keep agents enthusiastic about and committed to the customer contact cause. These managers, rather than simply chalk employee burnout and alienation up to the "nature of the call center beast," fight every day to reduce—or, better, prevent—the feelings of stress, futility and worthlessness that send so many agents packing.

"Save the Agent" Strategies

Here is a list of some key practices and programs that have helped to significantly lower incidents of agent burnout at a wide range of call centers.

• **Feasible and fair performance objectives.** Nobody will argue that call centers need to have formal service level and performance goals in place to help ensure customer satisfaction and to control costs. But agents at many centers will argue that management has set them up for failure by implementing objectives that are nearly impossible to achieve and/or that focus on factors that are out of their control.

Such complaints from staff—and the resulting burnout/turnover—have led many progressive call center managers to redefine the entire performance measurement process in their centers. One common trend is that managers are placing less emphasis on—and even doing away with—certain purely quantitative metrics like "calls handled per hour" and "average talk time" that have historically ruled the performance measurement roost. These call centers have acknowledged that such metrics are often influenced by things that agents can't control (i.e., call volumes and types), and thus don't always paint an accurate picture of how well each agent is doing their job.

According to Jeanne Dorney, manager of Rodale Inc.'s call center in Emmaus, Pa., moving from a mostly numbers-based environment to one where quality and relationship building are valued was the best thing she could have done to stem staff burnout.

"We don't measure the number of things that agents do in any particular span of time," Dorney explains. "Instead, we look at how well they do those tasks. I believe that was a big step in reducing the pressure on agents to perform."

• **Intriguing off-phone tasks and projects.** Supportive call center professionals are learning that agents who live merely by the phone, die by the phone. To dramatically lower the death count, these managers are tapping the various capabilities of their staff and creating more diverse opportunities for them.

Granted, the first priority in these call centers remains handling customer contacts efficiently, but agents are being given the chance to show that they can do much more. For example, many managers have implemented agent-led task forces responsible for making improvements to key processes, such as recruiting/hiring, monitoring, incentives, etc.

Laura Sikorski, managing partner of the consulting firm Sikorski-Tuerpe & Associates, has seen the positive impact that agent-led task forces and project teams has had at many call centers. "If you give agents the opportunity to change the system, you'll be amazed at how motivated and committed they will become," Sikorski says.

To battle burnout among the call center's most experienced staff, some managers have created special programs where these individuals are empowered to share their skills and knowledge. Peer mentoring, where veteran staff are paired with new-hires to assist them in training and on the job, is a prime example. And one that works, according to Dr. Jan Northup Kratochwill, president of Management Training Systems Inc., who has helped several call centers implement "mentoring for success" programs. As she explains, "The mentor gets power, prestige and visibility; the protégé gets confidence; and the organization gets cost-effective training and increased productivity."

Another way in which many managers have added diversity to the agent position is by letting them occasionally use their individual talents on the job, away from the phones. For example, some managers have offered agents with strong writing skills the chance to write for the company newsletter, or even create a call-center specific newsletter. Others look to the "artists" among their staff to create posters and decorations for special events or contests in the call center. The opportunities for tapping agents' creative talents are endless, and priceless, says Tracy Laycock, general manager of the renowned training consulting firm Phone Pro. "Find out what interests [agents] and put them to work. The agent's job satisfaction will increase, customers will be happier and the manager will spend less time conducting interviews due to high turnover."

• **Creative and continuous agent recognition/awards.** Top call centers today understand that "15 minutes of fame" just isn't enough to stem burnout among hard-working staff. That's why managers at these centers spend a lot of time looking for creative ways to reward and recognize agents on a frequent basis.

Chapter 5

Such dedication to agent appreciation is what led to the multifaceted "Blue Diamond" recognition program at Independence Blue Cross (IBC) in Philadelphia. Under Blue Diamond—a monthly program—agents receive gift certificates and accolades for demonstrating excellence in areas ranging from attendance and punctuality to accuracy and professionalism. Agents who "go above and beyond the call of duty"—which may include helping out with training, effectively handling a special project, or suggesting a way to help improve operations—also receive special recognition each month. Once a year, top Blue Diamond winners are invited to a recognition breakfast, where they receive a certificate of achievement, an American Express gift certificate and a gold coin. Since its introduction in 1996, the Blue Diamond program has been very successful, especially among agents who are making the call center their career, says Hank Kearney, senior director of member services for IBC.

An increasingly popular trend among call centers is to place incentive programs directly into the hands of the employees themselves. For example, at AT&T Broadband (with numerous call centers nationwide), managers asked a team of top-performing agents to develop a recognition and reward system as part of the company's aim to "infect the center with enthusiasm," explains Rhonda Mohacsi, director of the customer call group for the company's Los Angeles market. "We sat down with [the agents], gave them the budget and the objectives, and asked them to come up with ideas. They've done a tremendous job developing a program to motivate themselves and their peers." The program features a variety of games and contests that regularly reward both individual and team achievement.

Many smaller call centers—with often miniscule budgets—rely on a number of fun, often informal, ways to show agents how much their work is appreciated. For instance, Charlotte Baptie, call center manager of Gordon Food Service in Ontario, Canada, has become an expert on stretching a tight budget to battle burnout. She and her staff have introduced a dynamic little incentive program that features a wide variety of small monthly awards and prizes (mostly food certificates and products donated by corporate partners) as well as kudos on office bulletin boards. According to Baptie, "Even the smallest recognition is important." But that doesn't mean her call center doesn't know how to recognize agents in a big way, too. Each year the center stages its annual agent "Appreciation Week" that is filled with games, food, prizes and decorations. Baptie says that they aren't able to spend a lot on supplies for the special week, but that "Everyone looks forward to it."

- **Social events held both in-house and outside the call center.** Even in call centers that feature a formal team environment, feelings of loneliness and alienation among agents are common due to the independent nature of the job. With agents' primary responsibility being to stay seated at their workstation and handle customer contacts, there is often little time for informal visits and chats with colleagues.

Many call center managers have taken big steps toward changing the "anti-social" aspect of the agent position, organizing events that help to bring staff together in a fun, relaxing setting. Common examples include monthly or bimonthly birthday celebrations that are held in-house and that honor all agents born during the month(s) in question, and "pot-luck" lunches or dinners where each agent brings a dish to the call center and is given the opportunity to meet/spend time with other agents.

Of course, in-house celebrations can be tricky because of the need to have a large percentage of staff on the phones at any given time. That's why some managers seek to foster agent camaraderie outside the call center. This is often done via dinners at nearby restaurants, or by organizing weekly or monthly events such as "pub night" or "bowling night." In several call centers, the agents themselves have taken over the responsibility of creating the social calendar, thus further enhancing the bond among workers.

- **"Wellness" strategies.** If there were such a thing as The Call Center Employee Olympics, agents at companies like Wisconsin Power and Light (now Alliant Energy) and Duke Power would likely take home the lion share of the medals. These call centers, as well as a growing number of others, have implemented full-fledged wellness strategies and special amenities to help keep agents healthy, energized and mentally alert.

As part of its innovative "Keep Well" program, Alliant Energy provides agents with "quiet rooms" filled with books, a CD player, comfortable couches, as well as vending machines containing healthy snack options. One room is even equipped with exercise machines. In addition, all agents are provided with ample 7x7 workstation cubicles that are equipped with fully adjustable chairs, footrest/armrests and workstation tabletops. To ensure that agents understand the importance of good ergonomics, the call center brings an occupational therapist in to work with each new training class and show them how to adjust their workstation equipment. The company's investment has more than paid off; since introducing the "Keep Well" program, staff absenteeism and turnover has dropped while productivity has risen, says management.

Managers at Duke Power have seen similar results since renewing their focus on agent health and well-being. The wellness strategy is highlighted by a "Quality Life Center"—an exercise facility where agents can work out job stress around the clock. Agents also receive regular "ergonomic assessments" to ensure their optimum comfort and performance on the job.

• **Formal skill/career paths.** When staffing services firm Manpower conducted a study to identify the key motivators for call center staff, topping the list were "the chance to learn new skills" and "to be offered continuous new challenges and support for personal growth." Numerous progressive managers have answered their agents' call for more opportunities by implementing viable skill and/or career paths in the call center. Such paths encourage agents to continually expand their capabilities and knowledge, and thus increase their value to the call center and the organization.

While several call centers have effectively implemented a formal career path—which typically feature a wide range of positions ranging from new-hire all the way up to supervisor or manager—many centers aren't large enough to effectively maintain such programs, and instead have opted for the skill path route. Pitney Bowes' skills-based pay program provides a prime example of such a venture. The program, implemented several years ago at the company's Mailing

Systems Division, features 50 skill blocks that are divided into three major categories: 1) core, 2) advanced, and 3) expert. To attain a specific skill, agents complete a small training module featuring self-paced and on-the-job instruction, as well as a certification test. For every new skill attained, agents receive a bump in salary.

And the call center receives a happier, more empowered, more committed employee.

"We have more control over our future now," says Joney Ashley, an agent at Pitney Bowes' call center in Spokane, Wash. "We can take training, upgrade our skills and take a test to prove we are up to speed. If you know the plan up-front and you know there are opportunities, you're more inclined to stay at the company."

• **Stress management training.** While the strategies and practices covered in this article have helped many companies stave off agent burnout, there is no way to eliminate stress entirely from the dynamic and fast-paced call center environment. This fact has inspired some managers to introduce training that helps agents effectively deal with their stress. Such training is often led by specialized consultants and covers the common causes and effects of job stress, as well as methods for controlling it. The best programs seek agent input regarding specific stress factors in the call center, and encourage agents to suggest ways to reduce or eliminate those factors.

Stress awareness and management training is highly effective because it clearly shows employees that the organization is aware of and concerned about the problem of on-the-job stress, explains Cary Cherniss, professor of applied psychology at Rutgers University. A good stress management course, Cherniss says, shows agents that managers "don't ignore [the problem of stress], dismiss it or downplay it."

Combating the Negative Effects of Job Stress in the Call Center
by Susan Hash

Stress is prevalent in the workplace. In call centers, in particular, the daily stress associated with workplace demands can be further magnified by the anxiety of being constantly under fire from callers.

Job stress in the call center can be divided into two key categories, says Stephen Coscia, customer service trainer and author of *Tele-Stress*. There are internal causes—those that call centers inflict on their agents, which include workload, call volume and unsupportive supervisors, and external causes—which are imposed by customers calling into the center.

"Stress results when agents' resources aren't equal to the demands of the situation," says Kris R. Ludwigsen, Ph.D., senior clinical psychologist for Kaiser Permanente in Northern California, and a fellow of the American Psychological Association. "That can be their perceived resources and perceived demands. Stress also comes from conflicting demands in the workplace or from uncertainty about what one's role is, as well as from an individual's inability to discharge the tension or let go."

Ludwigsen adds that call center agents can also experience a type of "caretaker stress" from constantly trying to meet the needs and demands of callers.

The National Institute for Occupational Safety and Health (NIOSH) pegs the early-warning signs of job stress as headaches, sleep disturbances, difficulty concentrating, job dissatisfaction and low morale. For the organization, stressful working conditions are associated with increased absenteeism, tardiness, low performance and disability claims.

Work stress "imposes enormous and far-reaching costs on workers' well-being and corporate profitability," says NIOSH Director Linda Rosenstock. "Some of those costs are avoidable. Research and experience tell us that certain factors, such as heavy work load, conflicting or uncertain job responsibilities and job insecurity are stressors across organizations and that the risk of job

Chapter 5

stress can be reduced through smart, strategic action."

A study of call center workers by the Australian Services Union identified the five most frequent factors contributing to stress in the call center as: rude customers, call monitoring/recording, equipment failure, bad telephone and computer equipment, and unsupportive managers.

The study also found that lack of communication and encouragement from managers, the call center technology and a need for more training and support are major causes of stress among agents.

How can you tell if an agent is stressed out? Tracking individual statistics can highlight drops in performance that might indicate job burnout. Coscia suggests keeping an eye on those agents who have a disproportionate amount of escalated calls, those with an increase in tardiness, those who are not logged into the

---

THE IMPACT OF STRESS

The Australian Services Union conducted a survey of 658 union and non-union call center workers. Key findings revealed:

- 88% of respondents find their job and workplace stressful.
- Stress caused almost a third of workers to take time off work; the median length was five days.
- Just over a third believed they received insufficient communication and encouragement from managers.

The Families and Work Institute's 1997 *National Study of the Changing Workforce* reported:

- Today's jobs are more demanding—employees spend an average of 44 hours a week working. In addition, many workers say they have to work very fast (68%) and very hard (88%).
- Nearly one-fourth of all employees often or very often felt nervous or stressed; 13% often or very often had difficulty coping with the demands of everyday life; 26% often or very often felt emotionally drained by their work; and 36% often or very often felt used up at the end of the workday.

---

queue for the appropriate number of hours, and agents with low problem-resolution rates.

Organizational Changes that Can Lower Burnout

According to NIOSH, a combination of organizational change and stress management is the most useful approach for preventing stress at work.

In its report, *Stress at Work*, NIOSH highlights several organizational characteristics associated with a low-stress, high-productivity environment. Those include:

- Recognition of staff for good work performance.
- Opportunities for career development.
- A culture that values the individual worker.
- Management actions that are consistent with organizational values.

Organizational changes suggested by NIOSH include ensuring that the workload is in line with workers' capabilities and resources; designing stimulating, meaningful jobs; defining workers' roles and responsibilities clearly; giving workers the opportunity to participate in decisions about their jobs; improving communication; providing opportunities for social interaction among workers; and establishing work schedules that are compatible with demands and responsibilities outside of the job.

Train Supervisors to Be "Emotional Coaches"

A pivotal component in agent stress levels is the frontline supervisor's attitude toward call center stress.

"The most important factor in ameliorating stress is the supervisor," says Cary Cherniss, professor of applied psychology at Rutgers University. He says that the most effective stress management programs target supervisors more than the frontline staff.

"Research shows that workers who deal well with stress tend to have supervisors who are aware of and concerned about the problem of stress experienced by their staff. They don't ignore it, dismiss it or downplay it. And they're very effective in communicating that concern to their employees," he says.

In addition, the more effective supervisors are those who are good coaches—both in terms of providing information, strategies and helpful suggestions to agents, as well as providing suggestions for coping with the stress.

Besides having an understanding of the amount of stress on call center agents, supervisors should be able to identify the signs of burnout in individuals, and offer those agents breaks from the work—from a few minutes off the phones to a few days depending on the severity, says Ludwigsen.

Coscia adds that supervisors can also alleviate work stress by identifying the most common, repetitive calls coming into the center, and exploring other ways to handle those transactions, such as posting FAQs, using fax-back systems or offering access via the interactive voice response (IVR) system.

Ensure Performance Measures Don't Add to Work Anxiety

Is it possible to balance your agents' mental well-being with the need to meet service levels and track performance? Some call centers have been very successful at redefining how agent performance is measured.

A few years ago, publisher Rodale Inc.'s call center moved from a transactional environment to a relationship environment. "We don't measure the number of things that agents do in any particular span of time. Instead, we look at how well they do those tasks. I believe that was a big step in reducing the pressure on agents to perform," says Call Center Manager Jeanne Dorney.

The call center's quality program measures agents' performance in areas like professionalism and attendance. "They're not measured on anything that's not within their control," Dorney says.

Sento Corp., a technical support outsourcer in American Fork, Utah, has turned its agents' performance measurement into a recognition program in which agents receive daily profit-and-loss statements, says the company's Chief Morale Officer Kirk Weisler. In fact, agents are educated on the basics of running the business—they know the center's overhead (down to what their cubicles cost), the company's gross margins and profit margins. They're also told of

HOW TO HANDLE STRESS-RELATED COMPENSATION CLAIMS

What happens when an agent files a job-related mental stress workers' compensation claim? What accommodations should managers make for the individual?

Charles Goldstein, a California-based attorney who specializes in labor and employment law, offers this advice:

- First, be sure to check the individual's medical information to make yourself aware of their specific limitations. "You don't want to treat them differently or in any way that can be considered retaliatory," Goldstein says. "You don't want to violate the Americans with Disabilities Act, which is far more costly because then you can be sued for actual compensatory and punitive damages."

- Get medical verification that the agent can perform the essential duties of the job—with or without a reasonable accommodation.

- Determine whether or not the accommodation is truly reasonable or if it will create an undue hardship. Often, Goldstein says, companies create "non-jobs" for the employees who file claims—while the rest of the staff are left to carry the workload, which creates departmental resentment. "The law does not require you to permit people to have non-jobs with no economic value under the guise of protecting them from being discriminated against because they have a disability," he explains. "So if you have somebody with a stress claim, make certain that the medication that they're taking does not in any way interfere with their ability to do the essential duties of the job." The essential duties are defined as those core duties that give the job economic value (not peripheral duties).

- If you find that the duties the individual can perform have no value in your call center, you don't have to allow them to come back to work until they have confirmation from a doctor who will certify they can do the job with or without a reasonable accommodation and perform the essential duties. "Don't allow someone to present you with a 'grade school' release that says: 'Johnny can return to work.' That doesn't help you; it doesn't specify if they can perform the essential duties of the job," he says.

the specific revenue associated with every type of call they take. The daily reports show them how many calls, emails and chats they've handled, plus the dollar amount associated with it.

"This daily feedback is a daily recognition statement," says Weisler. "We focused on the way we presented it—you don't want to just give people numbers; you want to show them a picture. If people can see, graphically, a meaningful picture of their performance on a daily basis, they have immediate control over it. The performance is really theirs, they deserve to know what it is."

A Sense of Control Improves Morale, Cuts Stress

The American Psychological Association reports a universal cause of job stress is the feeling of powerlessness. And the more highly stressed occupations are those marked by the need to respond to others' demands and timetables with little control over events.

At Sento, call center agents are in charge of their own raises. Those who demonstrate a level of performance above the set requirements for 90 days can bump up their hourly pay by $1.25.

According to Weisler, the lack of ambiguity on how well agents are doing or whether or not they'll get a raise eliminates the anxiety over performance and work control.

"That doesn't mean agents won't get stressed when they get a really irate customer," he says. "You still have that. But you don't have to give your people a hard break with the way the work's set up." Sento also sends call queue statistics to agents' desktops so they can determine on their own when to take their breaks.

Elements of a Formal Stress Prevention Program

The Office of Disease Prevention and Health Promotion conducted a national study which found that only 37 percent of workplaces offered employees some type of stress management or reduction activities.

According to NIOSH, the process for developing a formal stress prevention program involves three steps: problem identification, intervention and evalua-tion. At a minimum, preparation for a stress prevention program should include:

- Building general awareness about job stress (causes, costs, control).
- Getting top management commitment and support for the program.
- Incorporating agent input and involvement in all phases of the program.
- Establishing the technical capacity to conduct the program (staff training, bringing in job-stress consultants, etc.).

Besides developing a formal program that involves education and assess-ment, there are other methods that managers have found to be effective at reducing call center stress:

- In addition to its onsite fitness center, Rodale has set aside "quiet rooms" that agents can use as a stress-free zone, says Dorney.
- Getting a break from the daily grind also helps agents to re-energize after a peak call volume period. "For every difficult period we go through, we try to give something back to the agents," Dorney says. For instance, the call center might shut down the phones on a Saturday after a stressful period to allow

---

A HEALTHY CALL CENTER CHECKLIST

Changing your call center environment from stressful to healthy takes time and commitment. You can begin by targeting those changes that will have the highest impact on stress reduction. The following list from the Job Stress Network are broad organizational goals that you can focus on breaking down into specific programs. Healthy organizational change includes changes that:

- Will increase agents' autonomy or control.
- Will increase the skill level of agents.
- Will increase levels of social support (both supervisory and peer).
- Will improve physical working conditions.
- Will make a healthy use of technology.
- Will provide job security and career development.
- Will provide healthy work schedules.
- Will improve the personal coping mechanisms of agents.

---

agents to work offline.

• The American Psychological Association suggests that managers ensure that every agent have a specific written job description—one that they help to write. Being able to negotiate job duties can go a long way toward dispelling a sense of powerlessness over their jobs.

• If you have a recreation budget for the call center, Sento's Weisler suggests giving your agents control over the funds. "If your center has a budget for pizza, the managers shouldn't be in charge of it," he says. "Give the budget to your people. Let them order pizza when they anticipate stressful periods."

• Make sure agents are well-prepared for difficult calls. "Have protocols on hand that agents can refer to which outline the steps to take under various stressful circumstances," says Ludwigsen.

• Try to cultivate a feeling of camaraderie among your agents. Foster a team environment rather than a competitive one in which agents are pitted against each other to reach performance goals.

• Set up a peer-to-peer recognition system in which agents can reward one another. "We keep on hand plenty of movie tickets, free lunch tickets to our cafeteria and video rental certificates for on-the-spot recognition," says Dorney.

Stress Prevention ROI

It's difficult to measure the specific results associated with stress reduction programs in the call center—unless you look at agent attrition rates.

"We think it's reflected in the retention of our agents," says Dorney. "Our turnover is well below industry standards, even though there have been several new call center openings in our area. Our people are staying, so we must be doing something right."

Sento's Weisler believes that stress prevention should be an industrywide mission. "Our industry has become known as the sweatshop of the new millennium. I don't want to be a part of that," he says. "I don't want to deal with stress. I want to set up an environment where the stress has been dealt with before it occurs."

Chapter 6: Develop an Effective Turnover Plan

While reducing staff churn is paramount to call center success, eliminating it entirely is not. In fact, doing so could even be harmful. Internal turnover—where agents take their skills to other areas of the enterprise—can help the organization improve its overall performance. The key is to effectively plan for and manage turnover.

"Designed Turnover": A Different Approach to Retention
by Elizabeth A. Ahearn

As call center leaders, we continually spend our energy trying to entice agents to stay by offering incentive programs that include contests, playrooms and even food. Despite these "perks," the average turnover in call centers across the country still hovers at around 35 percent.

In an issue of *Fortune* magazine, Jac Fitz-enz of The ROI of Human Capital says, "The cost to replace an employee is the equivalent of at least six months of a non-exempt person's pay and benefits, and a minimum of one year's worth for a professional or manager."

Perhaps focusing on call center agent retention is not the answer. In fact, in some companies the call center serves as a portal to the rest of the organization with "designed turnover" as a strategy. These companies have been very successful in delivering consistent world-class service despite planned attrition and have positioned the call center as a respected and valued partner within the corporation.

The Type of Environment that Promotes Commitment

Companies that attempt to retain agents by merely developing more morale boosters (which may or may not work because the success of such programs is highly dependent on the company's brand recognition factor, senior leadership charisma and competition incentives) continually struggle with poor morale and/or unplanned turnover.

A survey conducted by The Radclyffe Group annually since 1994 confirms that call center leadership spends, on average, 80 percent of their time dealing with petty personnel and morale issues with agents. The fact is, the more perks we provide for agents, the higher the bar is raised in terms of their expectations for future programs.

Instead, I have found that taking a holistic approach to agent development and retention can create an intellectually rich environment while maintaining agent individualism and liberation, thereby resulting in commitment to the organization.

The Hay Group, in its 1999 *Employee Attitudes Study* of 300 companies throughout the country, defines commitment to the organization as the intention to stay with a company for the next five years at a minimum. The results of this study identified the characteristics that play a critical role in an agent's commitment:

- Opportunities to learn new skills (this does not mean new products)
- Coaching and feedback from immediate boss
- Ability of top management
- Type of work
- Recognition for a job well-done
- Respectful treatment
- Training
- Pay

The 1999 *Radclyffe Group Call Center Benchmarking Study* determined that agents enjoy working in an environment in which there is:

- **Effective communication**—including receiving the direction they need to be successful; timely feedback; having a clear understanding of standards and expectations; and being held accountable.

- **Trust**—leaders who are good role models and who do what they say they are going to do, provide followup feedback, are consistent in how they make decisions, are fair and equitable, and actively discourage triangulation.

- **Professional development**—creating an environment in which people are continually being intellectually challenged and stretched professionally along with methodical mastering of skills with appropriate measurements and recognition.

- **Job satisfaction**—the perception that individuals do make a difference to the company and its customers through their everyday work.

These two sources provide insight into common factors that are valued by the agents in a work environment. Based on both quantitative and qualitative data, agents want to work in a professional environment in which they are intellectually stimulated and are clear about their professional career path and exactly what it takes to get there. They want to receive coaching about what is important and will make a difference to them professionally. And they want to feel fulfilled in their jobs, just like we do as leaders.

A "HOLISTIC" APPROACH TO RETENTION MOTIVATES AGENTS

The holistic approach to agent retention is ongoing and focuses on methodical mastering of skills over time. Agents are motivated by this approach for several reasons:

- They have a plan on which to focus instead of focusing on entitlement issues (what they don't have, who takes a longer break, etc.).
- They can see their progress—where they were, what they have achieved and where they are going.
- They are clear about what they need to accomplish. There are no questions about what it takes to succeed and, therefore, there are no allegations of favoritism.
- Their perception of coaching is more positive than negative because they are being treated professionally and their coaches are focusing on professional development.
- This approach provides agents with a pathway to professional fulfillment— opportunities to learn new skills, opportunities to advance (including lateral movement) and coaching from their immediate manager.
- An inherent factor in working in a call center as an agent is the feeling of being out of control. This approach provides agents with a strong sense of control over professional development.
- This approach sends a strong message that "getting out of the call center" is not necessarily the goal, so that the call center is not considered an ancillary department in the organization. Talented staff actually come back to the department when they have achieved certain competencies in other areas.

Chapter 6

Ensure All Areas of the Firm Have Knowledgeable Staff

A few years ago, a major automobile manufacturer started taking a holistic approach in the pursuit of delivering world-class service to car owners. They have succeeded in providing that level of service and are continuously striving to maintain it.

They have a team of sophisticated leaders who understand the objectives and apply them conceptually. Considered a learning organization, it serves as a benchmark in the call center industry. They have implemented Designed Turnover Strategy™ (DTS), which has enabled them to leverage their internal talent and cultivate individuals as they progress through their long-term careers within the corporation. As a result, individuals move into the call center from other areas in the organization, move up and then back out to other areas, returning again at different stages of development.

This approach ensures that both the call center and other areas of the organization have knowledgeable staff at all times. While the specific approach is modified depending on each organization's needs, the basic strategy is the same:

• Create a competency model for each position within the call center. This document should define the necessary skills and behaviors and describe each level of performance (i.e., no indication of behavior, some indication, proficient or expert). Hire only those individuals who can demonstrate the critical competencies of the job.

• Create a professional career development model for each position within the organization. Identify where individuals can move both within the call center and externally. Ensure that there are places to move within the company and within the department. If opportunities for such movement do not currently exist, a partnering plan should be developed and "sold" within the organization.

• Create standards (minimum levels of performance) and expectations (based on skill level, knowledge and experience) for each job.

• Facilitate a skills assessment using the competency model (both self-assessment and manager assessment) for each individual in the organization.

- Create a professional development plan based on business objectives and agent interest. This document should include realistic timeframes for movement based on business needs and the individual's demonstration and application of the competencies required for the new position.

- Design and implement a "university-style" curriculum that is level-based. This curriculum should include courses specifically targeting core competencies development for the call center and each job within it, as well as electives that will enable staff to achieve their professional goals, which match the business needs.

A Holistic Approach Has Long-Term Benefits

Using a holistic approach provides a foundation and a strategy for creating an environment in which methodical mastering of skills over time will ensure an intellectually challenging workplace. In addition, it creates a pathway for strategically moving individuals to and from the department, while building credibility throughout the organization.

Companies that have implemented this type of program have had success in achieving long-term results in delivering world-class service and leveraging the corporation's talent. It has become obvious that using designed turnover as a strategy fosters a professional culture and provides a pathway to the desired results for each organization and individual within it in a way that simply relying on non-valued perks and playing games alone do not. The results of applying a holistic approach to employee retention will prove to be more long-lasting and far-reaching for the organization and its bottom line.

Consider Agent Turnover to be a Friend, Not a Foe

by John Carver

What's the most likely topic of conversation when two or more call center managers get together? New technology is sometimes discussed or debated. Good management practices may be shared. Benchmarking targets, first-call resolution, customer complaints, the Web, performance results... Some of these issues also may creep into the conversation, depending on how well the group members know each other.

But in a formal call center group meeting or in a subsequent social get-together, without fail, the topic of *employee turnover* will be raised, and usually in negative tones.

Agent Turnover Doesn't Have to Be Negative

Turnover, traditionally, has been viewed as a negative measure. The higher the turnover rate, the more call center management is perceived to be ineffective. High turnover causes higher recruiting, hiring and training expenses. Also, consider the cause and effect between turnover and morale: Does high agent turnover lead to poor call center morale or vice versa?

It doesn't have to be that way. Turnover can be viewed positively. Two years ago, our call center at the Bank of Montreal had a turnover rate of 100 percent. Last year, and so far this year, it's running at about 60 percent. But in our call center, turnover is encouraged, in fact, it's celebrated—the higher, the better. It's part of our company culture. And a week without a couple of promotions out of the call center is a rare one.

No, I haven't lost my mind. Let me explain: When we hire candidates for our call center, we hire people who are looking for a career, not just in the call center, but anywhere in our bank. We recognize that many applicants have higher ambitions, and that they may be applying for a call center agent position

Chapter 6

because they see it as a door opener. I talk with each new-hire orientation class and let them know that we're OK with that—we're here to give them a start, an entry into the Bank of Montreal. We give them a fantastic grounding in sales and service in the credit card business, where they master negotiation and communication skills, and then we send them on their way. The message is: Be successful in our call center and your management team will do all it can to help you move forward with your career.

We see ourselves as a human resource pool for our bank. I believe this strategy is worth considering in any call center in any industry. What better way to become well-versed in your business than to talk with 100 or more of your customers every day for a year or two?

Why Attrition Can Be Positive

If this strategy doesn't fit with your particular situation, there are many other good reasons to view turnover in a positive light. Here are a few to consider:

• **Attitude.** If your hiring is done right, new agents will bring positive attitudes to your center. We've found that new agents generally are very receptive to change and, as we all know, change is a way of life in call centers.

• **Enthusiasm.** Don't exclude students when hiring new agents. You may have to work their school hours into your schedule, but if you can accomplish this, you'll find that they're very receptive to flex hours, which is a plus for most call centers. Also, students are full of enthusiasm. How long has it been since you heard a positive buzz on your floor? Students do that for you. And a third, long-term plus... many will return to you when they have completed their education.

• **Training.** Constant turnover means new, fresh minds to challenge your training group—and challenged minds tend to think more creatively.

• **Morale.** Yes, staff morale can improve with high turnover. We've proven that concept in our call center. Although call centers typically are not expected to be the leading organization in staff morale metrics, our employee commitment index has been rated the 10th highest in our bank (out of 700 groups measured) and the highest of groups with more than 100 people.

There are several other good reasons to view turnover positively, but these, to me, are the most significant ones. The most important message I can provide is: "Start looking at, and talking about, turnover in a positive light." Be a leader in this regard. When the manager sets the climate, agents respond.

Chapter 6

Effective Planning for Turnover
by David Mitchell

Let's see a show of hands: How many of you work in call centers that aren't providing the desired level of service? How many of you feel you will always be short staffed? How many are fighting to explain why your call center hasn't achieved its targeted level of service? Take a closer look—the culprit may be turnover.

Often overlooked by many call centers in their business planning and staffing models, turnover occurs for many reasons: higher pay by competitors, relocation, burnout, job dissatisfaction, scheduling disputes, promotions, terminations and lifestyle changes. The impact turnover has on a company affects many areas. Turnover can't be controlled 100 percent, which leaves us with one solution... planning.

Planning for turnover can move your call center one step closer to meeting the service levels outlined in your business plans. But first, we must take a closer look at turnover in order to understand its components.

Natural and Unnatural Turnover

By categorizing turnover into two separate types—natural and unnatural—we can discover areas in which modifications can be made to reduce overall turnover.

Natural turnover consists of areas that are generally out of your control as a call center manager. They may include relocation, promotions, graduations and lifestyle changes. Generally, this type of turnover is continuous no matter what type of agent retention program you have in place. The lives of your agents change, and this results in turnover for the call center.

Unnatural turnover includes agents leaving for higher pay, conflicts with management, job dissatisfaction, scheduling disputes, burnout and unexpected terminations. These are the more controllable components of turnover, and you should attempt to reduce them if possible by modifying some of the business practices in your call center. If these components are high, and you do not make any policy changes or operational modifications, then you can expect unnatural turnover to continue at its current rate, or worsen.

Since natural turnover will always be present, turnover is rarely zero. Add to the equation unnatural turnover, and the end result is a negative effect on your staffing and service levels. If an area of your business affects performance in a negative manner and is predictable via statistics, it should be included in your planning.

To understand the specific components of turnover that affect your call center, answer the following questions:

- What do you consider natural and unnatural turnover at your center?
- What is the breakdown percentage of each component?
- What can you do to reduce unnatural turnover?

Turnover Dollars and Sense

Make no mistake about it, high turnover can be an expensive proposition for most call centers. When you add hiring and training costs, salaries, development tools and extended benefits packages, the high costs of turnover can be downright devastating.

If you can answer the following questions then you already have a good start on the effects of turnover on the budget performance of your call center. If these questions are new to you, then answering them will give you a better snapshot of your turnover environment and the associated costs:

1. What is your turnover rate (yearly, monthly, weekly, per training cycle)? How does it compare with that of your competitors? With the industry as a whole?

2. How much does turnover cost your call center?
   - human resources (interviewing, exit interview, hiring)
   - materials
   - training costs (agent and trainer salaries, facilities)
   - extended benefits

3. What effects does turnover have on your call center?

- quality of service
- customer perception
- burnout rate of agents

Quantifying the costs of turnover is important for your business planning. Considering cost can allow you to compare possible solutions to reduce turnover. A good method of pinpointing cost is to list the hiring-termination process step by step, starting with advertising and ending with the agent walking out the door, then tying a specific dollar amount to each step. You may realize that not addressing the issue of turnover in your call center costs you more than implementing a potential solution.

By proactively planning for turnover and its potential effects, you can reduce the negative effects on your call center. Call centers employ various methods to handle turnover; some are effective and some are not. In the examples that follow, we will take a look at how three hypothetical companies—Call Center A, Call Center B and Call Center C—handle turnover, and discuss the positive and negative aspects of each method.

CALL CENTER A

Environment: Call Center A handles turnover in a very common manner: reactionary. Their required staffing level for FTEs (full-time equivalents) is equal to their approved staffing level. This is not a problem in itself, but when combined with management's passive treatment of turnover it causes insufficient staffing and service levels.

The center rehires to attain its approved staffing level every eight weeks, which is also how long it takes to train a new class of agents. The turnover rate continues to occur during training, so Call Center A will only be at full staff for a short period of time. By the time a new class is ready to handle contacts, the call center will be understaffed once again, and the cycle is continuous.

Diagnosis: Call Center A will not be able to meet its staffing requirements as long as turnover and current business practices continue. In addition, turnover has a negative effect on staffing because new-hires in training are treated as fully trained agents handling contacts. Calculating staffing levels using trainees in this manner overstates the total number of qualified agents available to handle the contact volume.

As a result, senior management may ask the following questions: "If you are fully staffed, why aren't you reaching your goals? Since you are fully staffed, do you need to make the agents work harder?"

CALL CENTER B

Environment: Call Center B has taken a positive step toward planning for turnover. Managers have calculated turnover rates and prehire and train based on those turnover statistics. They have shown a commitment to maintaining their service level goals by allowing their average staffing levels to equal their required staffing level. They realize that they must have agents in the pipeline to fill openings since turnover is continuous.

Call Center B prehires to their predicted turnover level every eight weeks. As was the case with Call Center A, this is the amount of time needed to train a new class of agents. Turnover continues during training, so Call Center B will be overstaffed 50 percent of the time and understaffed 50 percent of the time. When a new class is ready to handle customers, the call center will be understaffed once again. This method is a continuous cycle.

Diagnosis: Call Center B has taken a proactive approach to turnover by planning ahead. It realizes that agents in training should not be counted among the total number of staff working to handle contact volume. The call center achieves its desired staffing level and, on average, meets its service level objectives.

The cost for Call Center B to operate is higher than that of Call Center A due to the cost of additional agents. A portion of the cost is recovered due to a reduction in turnover (resulting from less burnout and a lower occupancy rate), lower telecommunication carrier costs (due to a faster average speed of answer), and lower hiring/termination costs due to lower turnover.

Senior management may ask managers at Call Center B things like, "Why are your staffing costs so high? Why is the center understaffed 50 percent of the time?"

CALL CENTER C

Environment: Call Center C has an optimum system in place for handling turnover effectively and efficiently. It has modified its business practices to minimize costs while meeting its service level goals. Managers know the turnover rate and prehire and train based on those statistics. They use a "just-in-time" system of turnover replacement. This system enables Call Center C to reduce costs by lowering the number of prehires it has on staff. The center's goal is to perfectly time the departure of existing agents and replace them with new agents. By shortening the time spent training agents, using one-on-one coaching, computer-based training (CBT) and self-study, the call center is able to react more quickly when turnover occurs. Call Center C does not train new agents in a large group setting. The center leverages technology to break free from the structured class environment and use tailored training programs that are customized to each new agent's ability.

Diagnosis: Call Center C has structured its environment to eliminate the negative effects of turnover on staffing as much as possible. This allows it to lower the cost for additional agents (versus Call Center B) and meet its service level goals 100 percent of the time. Because these goals are met, Call Center C also receives the benefits of less turnover, in comparison to Call Center A, as a result of less burnout. In addition, the center incurs lower telecommunication carrier costs and lower hiring/termination costs. Call Center C has accepted that turnover will continue and that it is a natural element within a call center.

Lessons Learned

We can see there are several choices when dealing with turnover. The least effective method of handling turnover is to do nothing, as shown in the Call Center A example. Your service level may suffer the greatest if you take a totally reactionary approach. Studying Call Center B and C demonstrates that there are tradeoffs between other approaches. These tradeoffs include cost versus convenience and technology versus non-technology. Which type of call center are you, A, B or C?

An effective plan for dealing with turnover, if implemented correctly, can help minimize the negative impact that may result from turnover. Accepting that there are certain natural and unnatural components of turnover will allow you to embrace the concept that turnover planning must be part of any call center business strategy. By analyzing the costs associated with turnover, and the different types of turnover that exist within your call center, you can proactively customize a turnover plan that suits your environment.

Managing Internal Agent Attrition

by Greg Levin

"Other departments keep stealing my agents!" This is the familiar cry of many call center managers struggling to keep qualified frontline staff in place. These managers work hard to recruit, hire and train skilled agents only to see them trade their headset in for a desk job in Marketing or Finance within a few short months. Such rapid internal turnover places the call center in a perpetual hiring and training mode that results in high costs and often poor service due to a shortage in experienced agents.

"But is internal attrition of call center agents really a problem?" ask members of other departments who benefit from the call center's loss. What's wrong with new employees gaining a little experience through a brief call center stint and then moving on to help the organization in other capacities?

Nothing, except for the fact that the organization as a whole may benefit significantly more if agents spent more time honing their service skills before moving on to another department. The call center would win because it would be staffed with experienced agents who could provide excellent service. Other departments would win because they would gain more seasoned employees with a solid grasp of the nature of the company as a whole and—even more importantly—the needs and expectations of the organization's customer base. Additionally, the longer that agents remain in the call center, the better the chances are that they will become supervisors or managers, meaning that the center will continue to be run by veterans who truly understand the dynamic environment.

While early internal attrition (agents leaving within six months) is common in many call centers, it is erroneous to place the blame solely on managers of other departments. They are not "stealing" agents—rather, agents are choosing to leave the call center to work in these other areas. Why? According to several experts in the industry, it's because of the negative call center image that exists in many organizations—an image that is often fostered by senior management's lack of support of and respect for the call center and its importance.

"Often the problem stems from the organization's perception of the role of the call center," says Fay Wilkinson, senior partner for Questeq Learning Programs, a Canadian consulting firm specializing in service quality management. "The job of agent is often viewed as merely an entry-level position—that the sooner you get out of there, the quicker you will rise to be a star somewhere else in the company. This negative perception and lack of recognition of the call center's value starts with senior management and trickles down to the rest of the organization."

KEY PRACTICES FOR REDUCING INTERNAL CHURN

Here is a list of some of the practices that Adam Boornazian, Fay Wilkinson and other call center professionals suggest for building a solid culture that inspires agents to remain in the center for as long as possible:

- **Educate agents during training on the importance and value of their jobs and the role of the call center.** Ensure that they understand that they represent the voice of the entire enterprise to the customer and, thus, can have a significant impact on the company's overall success.
- **Tap agents' individual talents to enhance projects.** Many of your agents have skills that range far beyond handling contacts. Take advantage of their capabilities to improve the call center and to break up the monotony of phone work. For example, if you have an agent with artistic ability, ask him or her to design creative posters for use during training or contests.
- **Emphasize quality customer interaction over straight productivity measurements.** Encourage agents to focus more on building profitable relationships with customers than on meeting quotas for calls per hour or on completing a call within a recommended "talk time." Explain the importance of adhering to schedules to maintain service levels and satisfy callers, but don't govern the center with adherence measurements.
- **Involve experienced agents in training, mentoring and monitoring.**

Chapter 6

Using veteran agents to help carry out training and monitoring tasks increases their sense of value, adds variety to their jobs and enhances their supervisory skills. In addition, newer agents often respond better to coaching and feedback from a colleague than from a manager/trainer.

- **Implement creative incentive programs and innovative compensation practices.** Move beyond pizza parties and smiley-face pins to motivate and retain agents. Introduce a variety of fun incentives that inspire agents to improve their skills and knowledge. To enhance acceptance, ask for agents' suggestions and feedback when creating incentives. Consider a skills-based pay program that rewards agents financially for continual development in the call center. Also, be sure to examine internal pay disparities between the agent position and "similar" positions in other departments.

- **Create formal career paths within the call center.** Show agents what opportunities lie ahead for them in the call center. Create a formal career path that incorporates several agent "levels" or "tiers," as well as positions such as team leader, assistant supervisor, supervisor and senior supervisor. Include similar tiers at the management level. Provide training and counseling to assist all agents with moving up in the call center, and ensure that a pay increase accompanies each position "jump."

Strong Call Center Culture Captures Agents

The poor perception of the call center in many companies often causes call center managers to feel that they are fighting a losing battle, Wilkinson adds. Many of these managers develop a defeatist attitude and, consequently, do little to build a strong call center culture via effective leadership. This results in unhappy agents, high turnover and poor performance—reconfirming senior management's perception of the call center as a "necessary nuisance."

It's up to call center managers to change how the organization perceives the center. One of the most crucial steps is creating an environment that makes agents want to work there. Easier said than done? Sure, but many call center professionals have worked hard at instilling a strong sense of value in the work agents do, and have succeeded in stopping the mass employee exodus to other departments.

"We realize how important it is to have experienced staff—rather than just green new-hires—speaking to our customers," says Adam Boornazian, vice president of customer contact operations for USA Group, a student loan company with call centers in Fishers, Ind., and Chandler, Ariz. "We've worked hard at building a culture that entices agents to remain in the call center. Some of that involves catchy buzzwords and mission statements, but it has more to do with how much participation and decision-making power you extend to your agents. If agents feel that they are part of an important team and have an impact on the way things work around them, they are more likely to have an interest in the success of the call center and want to stay there."

Empowering agents, treating them with respect and adding diversity to their jobs is essential not only for overcoming the poor call center image present in many organizations; it's important because handling call after call can be very repetitive and often results in early agent burnout and turnover. The problem, Boornazian explains, is that many call centers focus too strongly on call statistics to please senior management, and not enough on involving agents in projects and decisions, or on creating career paths. "The primary message that agents at many call centers receive is, 'Get your butt on the phones and stay there for eight hours—we'll tell you when you can stand up and when to sit down,'" Boornazian says. It's no surprise, he adds, that agents in such an environment often visit human resources in search of openings in other departments.

Tenure Requirements Rouse Debate

Some call center managers are getting aggressive with internal agent turnover, implementing policies that require frontline staff to remain in the call center for at least a year or 18 months. This practice has received some criticism from opponents. "You can't keep agents in the call center, you have to do things that make them want to stay," says Questeq's Wilkinson. "If an agent isn't happy in the call center, and he has a contract saying he can't move to another department for a year or so, he's likely to seek employment outside, meaning the organization loses the employee altogether."

Dick Boyle, vice president of customer services for Aetna Retirement Services in Hartford, Conn., says his call center uses one-year tenure agreements with much success. "The [tenure agreement] is an effective way to help manage your valuable employee assets," says Boyle. "It's not like we lock them in a horrible working environment for a year. We train and empower agents; we provide good incentives. Agents like it here—many have been working for us for years. The one-year requirement is simply a way to let applicants and other departments know that the call center plays a crucial role and needs to hire and develop career-minded individuals."

Boyle adds that he will make a rare exception to the tenure rule if an agent is miserable in the call center and he feels that the agent would fit better in another department. "The call center is not a prison or a punishment—I want people who want to come to work," he says. "And the vast majority do."

Boyle is in the process of lobbying for a "second-year" clause that would require other departments to pay up to $6,000 (about half the training investment per agent) for hiring agents who have spent less than two years in the call center. "We're not saying that other departments will have to wait until the agent's second year is up, but they will have to pay a price that recognizes the amount of energy and effort it takes to bring these people to the company and train them, as well as the impact that losing such people has on the call center and on customer service."

Boyle is currently negotiating with human resources and senior management to get approval for his unique second-year stipulation. "We're talking about it now, and I believe it will go into place very soon," he says.

Wilkinson feels such practices smack of territorialism and do little to enhance relationships between the call center and other departments within the organization. "It doesn't sound to me like there is much partnering or cooperation going on between departments in that company," she says.

Boyle counters that he's not being territorial at all, rather that his minimum tenure policies and proposed "fines" will benefit the entire enterprise in the long run. "I'm not telling the other departments, 'Don't ever come near my reps!'" he explains. "On the contrary, I'm telling them, 'You want these people—they are very knowledgeable, skilled individuals—but give me two years to develop them and make them as valuable as possible to you and our organization as a whole.'"

Turn Lost Agents into Assets

While proactive and creative management is key for retaining agents, managers cannot expect to completely stop internal turnover from occurring. As a result, they must focus on making the most of lost agents' talent. Whether quality agents stay for six months or for five years, a resourceful call center manager can still benefit from their skills and knowledge even after they've moved on within the organization, says Wilkinson. She is a big proponent of maintaining strong working relationships with other departments and former agents to enhance new-hire training as well as contingency staffing in the call center.

"An experienced agent is a tremendous asset who possesses a wealth of knowledge," says Wilkinson. "Whenever such an employee leaves the call center to go to another department within the organization, it's a mistake for call center managers to simply wave goodbye and sulk. In progressive organizations, call centers can invite former agents back to assist in training and mentoring of new agents, or to help out on the phones during peak volume periods. These centers have learned to partner with other departments to make the most out of losing valued knowledge workers."

The Hartford Customer Services Group (HCSG) is one such call center. HCSG maintains a core contingency team made up of former agents who have moved on to other departments. The center relies heavily on these employees to maintain service levels when call volumes are high. "During busy seasons, we might use them on the phones for five hours a week or so," says Jay Minnucci, director of call center operations for HCSG in Fort Washington, Pa. "Former agents serve as very valuable contingency staff for us. I don't know how we'd get through our peak periods without them."

The call center's primary peak season occurs each year between November and February. Former agents are also used during other predictable heavy volume times, such as the day following a three-day weekend or the Monday after customers receive their billing notices. In addition, the call center may bring in a few former agents to help fill staffing gaps resulting from training sessions or other meetings that require existing agents to go offline. Minnucci adds that the former agents enjoy the job diversity that helping out in the call center provides.

Having former agents working in other departments not only can enhance contingency planning, it helps to ensure that those departments will better understand the unique call center environment. "It certainly doesn't hurt to have a few people in Marketing who used to work in the call center," says Wilkinson. "They know the importance of alerting the call center managers about new campaigns and such so that those managers can make the necessary staffing decisions."

Inspire Staff to Stay "Home"

With the market for qualified agents as tight as ever, retaining and developing existing staff is crucial for call centers to provide the high level of service customers expect in today's competitive business environment. While some internal attrition is inevitable—and even valuable—managers must not lazily succumb to the ritual of finding agents, training them up and shipping them out to other "more important" departments within a few months.

You can't force agents to stay, but you can provide the culture, creativity and career path that will inspire them to make the call center their home for as long as possible.

Chapter 6

Chapter 7: Laughing Matters

High agent turnover brings many call center professionals to tears. The satirical articles in this chapter should help stop the sobbing and bring a bit of a sinister smile to your face.

Waging War on Agent Retention

By Greg Levin

Despite the increasing levels of respect and esteem that call center agents have received in recent years, the little punks keep leaving. Even with managers implementing attractive incentives, creating empowerment opportunities and handing out reward plaques made with genuine imitation silver plating, front-line staff continue to view the front door of the call center as an exit leading to better things.

I say enough with the nice-guy approach to curbing turnover—it's time to get mean. Managers have already spent too much time trying to come up with innovative strategies intended to make hard-to-please agents feel good about sticking around. Instead, I suggest waging war on retention—implementing creative measures mired in slyness and deceit that virtually prohibit staff from escaping. It all comes down to a simple call center philosophy: If you can't beat 'em, cheat 'em to seat 'em.

HERE'S HOW:

• **Trick agents into signing lengthy employment contracts.** While four out of five HR experts feel that "minimum tenure" contracts are a bad idea, five out of five call center managers recently beat up those HR experts and told them to be quiet. The truth is, such contracts—which typically call for at least a one-year or 18-month commitment to the call center—are not very popular with agents, which is why snake-in-the-grass tactics are recommended to get the little headset hoodlums to sign them. This includes making them think the contract is actually a sign-up sheet for an upcoming company-paid field trip to Barbados, or a formal petition for a window in the call center.

As long as you're going out of your way to deceive agents, you might as well make it worth the trouble and sucker them into a longer-than-usual call center commitment. For example, instead of a mere one- or two-year contract, create an agreement that requires each agent to remain in the call center until the Pope gets married, the USA wins a soccer World Cup, or your CEO starts flying coach.

Chapter 7

• **Scare off prospective employers.** I realize that many managers have too much class and grace to blatantly deceive agents via such sneaky contracts as previously suggested, but those managers probably don't read my column. Nonetheless, if you are turned off by my first recommendation, consider a less extreme method of turnover reduction that simply involves making agents appear less desirable to other organizations. Three key tactics are recommended: 1) tattooing "Anarchy Rules" on each agent's forehead (this is most easily accomplished while agents are in a deep sleep; i.e., during weekly team meetings); 2) sending local companies a group photo of your frontline staff with the caption, "Wanted for Murder" in big letters beneath it; and 3) placing heaps of raw garlic on all pizzas brought into the call center.

If, for some reason, you still receive a call from a prospective employer seeking a reference check on one of your current agents, pretend at first not to recognize the employee's name and then after a while say, "Ah yes, yes, I almost forgot about him—what with the extensive leave of absence he was forced to take due to that fungus problem…"

• **Break their will.** To become a true expert in employee retention, it's not enough to merely have a lot of self-confidence, you need to ensure that agents don't. Studies have shown that employees who don't believe in themselves are five times less likely to leave a company, and 10 times less likely to leave the parking lot. Thus, the more fear and feelings of self-doubt you can instill in agents, the more available they will be to satisfy your customers.

There are a number of effective ways to shatter your staff's self-confidence. One of the best entails showing each agent a video featuring somebody who looks exactly like their mother telling them that, if they ever left the call center, they would amount to less than nothing. Be sure that the script includes such lines as: "You never were very sharp" and "If only I hadn't smoked and drunk so much when I was pregnant with you."

Another great way to destroy employees' confidence in finding alternative employment is to stage a mock job fair staffed with actors who do nothing but point at your agents and giggle.

• **Be painfully bureaucratic.** All agents have to go through a rigorous application and interview process before coming on board the call center. Why not force them to go through a similar process when they want to leave? For instance, make "applicants" fill out complex and lengthy "Request for Exit" forms in triplicate using a broken pen and their left hand. Once they complete these forms, thank them for applying and let them know that the decision-making process normally takes anywhere from two to seven years. It's also a good idea to conduct interviews with each applicant to find out why they want to leave and what their plans are. At the end of the interview, tell them that you are sorry, but that you feel they simply don't have what it takes to succeed outside the call center.

Author's note: Despite the title of this article, I would like to emphasize that I have always been a devout pacifist who prefers peaceful solutions to all problems. If this article has upset you in any way, I would be happy to talk to you about it and, if necessary, flog you publicly until you see my point.

Chapter 7

Turnover Reduction Practices
by Greg Levin

If I had a dime for every time I heard a call center manager say, "Our turnover rate is high, but that's expected in this industry," I could buy a lot of quarters. It's no secret that turnover plagues many call centers. But too many managers simply accept this as "the nature of the industry," something which can not be avoided—like death or ACD-vendor press releases. Well, I think it's a cop-out. There are plenty of creative ways to reduce turnover in call centers, and managers need to start focusing on these innovative methods, or send me $4,250 cash to help them do so.

But first, some free suggestions. The following turnover reduction practices are guaranteed to help you hold on to your valuable staff and to increase over-all morale in the call center. If your agents don't respond enthusiastically to these methods, you should consider firing them immediately.

• **Make it *really* worth their while to stay.** Employees who feel valuable will not leave the call center, except hopefully to bathe and feed their pets on occa-sion. Pay agents what they are worth. If you are unsure what they are worth, ask their mothers. Provide attractive bonuses for superior performance (by the agents, not their mothers). For instance, if an agent receives high monitoring scores on three straight calls, buy them a timeshare in Aspen. But don't wait for agents to perform outstandingly before recognizing they exist. I'm not just talk-ing about giving them flowers or chocolates on their birthday—flowers die and chocolates can get lodged in the back of agents' throats, making it difficult for them to offer additional products and services to customers. If you truly want to reduce turnover, you have to really recognize your agents' existence. For example, send them to Paris on their birthday, but be sure to schedule them for the late shift the following day as jet-lag can impede performance. Or have the agent's bust sculpted out of marble once he or she has been with the call cen-ter for a year. The above suggestions may seem costly, but pale in comparison to the costs of re-recruiting, rehiring and retraining. (OK, OK, marble is expensive—try soapstone if budget is a big issue.)

- **Play motivational tapes in the restrooms.** Inspiring your agents to do a great job on the phones is essential for battling attrition, so why not use every free moment to do so? Agents may view the playing of motivational tapes in the restroom as strange at first, but will usually embrace it once they realize it isn't the toilet that's talking to them. An example of an effective call center lavatory message is, "You are the voice of the company; you can make a difference; you can raise our service level—now go wash your hands and return to your workstation." Shorter, more catchy messages such as, "Zip up your pants and do t—he call center dance!" will also do the trick.

- **Show alarming videos about job-scarcity during exit interviews.** Agents who have decided to leave the call center will often be emotionally vulnerable during the exit interview. It's up to you to take full advantage of their weakened psychological state and bombard them with frightening images of jobless, homeless, hungry people. To really get their attention, concoct your own video showing cold, shivering people wearing headsets while wandering city streets in search of workstations. If these tactics fail to cause the agent to reconsider and stay on with the company, let him or her go. You don't want somebody so callous handling your valued customers, unless he or she takes billing calls.

- **Get a big guy named Vinny to "counsel" agents who are thinking about quitting.** Sometimes all it takes for agents to reconsider their resignation is to hear how valued their work is from a respected authority figure. Other times, it takes threats of dismemberment from a thug in leather. If you find that you have to resort to the latter for purposes of turnover reduction, and are looking for leads, consult your local loan shark or visit Brooklyn and throw a stone in any direction. Hiring hit-men to reduce attrition may seem unnecessarily violent, but no more so than your trainer's reaction when she finds out she must cancel her vacation to the Bahamas to teach the ropes to another group of "potential service stars."

- **Stop hiring people.** Few can argue that it's difficult for staff turnover to increase if there aren't any people left to leave. Therefore, every time an agent quits, consider replacing him or her with an automated attendant. Automated attendants are never late to work, require no monitoring feedback and rarely spill soda on keyboards. However, 100 percent automation should be viewed as a last-resort option to reducing turnover, not only because of customers' demand for live-answer, but because Christmas parties at call centers staffed only with VRUs tend to be uneventful.

Chapter 7

Index

Publication Dates

How to Reach the Publisher

We would love to hear from you! How could this book be improved? Has it been helpful? No comments are off limits! You can reach us at:

Mailing Address: Call Center Press, a division of ICMI, Inc.
P.O. Box 6177
Annapolis, MD 21401

Telephone: 410-267-0700, 800-672-6177

Fax: 410-267-0962

Email: icmi@icmi.com

Web site: www.icmi.com

About Incoming Calls Management Institute

ICMI Inc. is a global leader in call center consulting, training, publications and membership services. ICMI's mission is to help call centers (contact centers, help desks, customer care, support centers) achieve operational excellence and superior business results. Through the dedication and experience of its team, uncompromised objectivity and results-oriented vision, ICMI has earned a reputation as the industry's most trusted resource for:

- Consulting
- Seminars
- Publications
- Management Tools
- Conferences and Networking Events
- Professional Membership

Based in Annapolis, Maryland, ICMI was established in 1985 and was first to develop and deliver management training customized for call centers. Through constant innovation and research, ICMI's training has become the industry's gold standard, and is recommended by 99.3% of those managers who have experienced its value first-hand. Over the years, ICMI has become the industry's leading provider of membership services with an impressive line-up of call center management resources, including instant access to prominent research, expert advice and career development tools, and a networking forum that spans more than 40 countries worldwide. ICMI is not associated with, owned or subsidized by any industry supplier—its only source of funding is from those who use its services. For more information about ICMI, visit www.icmi.com, or call 800-672-6177 (410-267-0700).

Author Biographies*

Elizabeth Ahearn is President and CEO of The Radclyffe Group, a performance improvement consulting firm. Liz is a speaker and author in the service industry, and has held call center leadership positions at Automatic Data Processing, IMS North America, the Pepsi-Cola Co. and Levi Strauss & Co.

Barbara Bauer is Vice President of the Omnia Group, an employee selection and management consulting firm based in Tampa, Fla.

Jean Bave-Kerwin is a Certified Associate of ICMI and President of JBK Consulting, which focuses on the needs and challenges of call centers in the government and non-profit sectors.

Seymour Burchman is a Principal at Sibson & Co. He helps companies to more effectively use human capital to support their business strategies and increase shareholder value.

John Carver is the former Senior Manager, Sales & Service Call Centre, Bank of Montreal, MasterCard. In addition, John was a winner of the 1999 Global Call Centre Manager of the Year Award.

*Author information is current for the publication date of the article (see page 171).

Michelle Cline is a Vice President for FurstPerson, an organization specializing in helping clients to find, hire and keep call center employees.

Susan Hash is the Editor-in-Chief of *Call Center Management Review.* She has been a business journalist/writer for more than 15 years, and has received several notable journalism awards for reporting on the customer service industry.

Sharon Jordan-Evans, President of the Jordan Evans Group, is an author, speaker, executive coach and workplace consultant. Sharon is a Professional Certified Coach, prominent speaker and co-author of *Love 'Em or Lose 'Em: Getting Good People to Stay,* and *Love It, Don't Leave It: 26 Ways to Get What You Want at Work.*

Beverly Kaye is President of talent management company Career Systems International. She is the author of the classic career development book, *Up is Not the Only Way,* and co-author of *Love 'Em or Lose 'Em: Getting Good People to Stay,* and *Love It, Don't Leave It: 26 Ways to Get What You Want at Work.*

Roger Kingsland is Managing Partner of Kingsland Scott Bauer Associates, Pittsburgh, Pa.-based architects specializing in research-based design of call centers.

Greg Levin is the Creative Projects Specialist for ICMI. He is the former editor of *Call Center Management Review*, and author of ICMI's *Call Center Humor* book series.

Julia Mayben is a freelance writer based in Annapolis, Md. She is a regular contributor to *Call Center Management Review*, and is co-author of *Call Center Management on Fast Forward*.

David Mitchell is the Network Services Manager for the Telephone Banking Center at Old Kent Financial Corporation in Grand Rapids, Mich. He oversees the coordination of telecommunications and information systems in the call center, as well as staffing and scheduling of personnel.

Anita O'Hara has been in call center management for more than 16 years, most recently as VP of Customer Services for Urban Media. She has held assignments with MediaOne, GTE Wireless and AT&T.

Debra Schmitt is a Senior Consultant at Sibson & Co. Debra develops and implements effective people strategies and practices that improve an organization's return on human capital.

Jennifer A. Wilber is Vice President of Training and quality assurance for National Service Direct Inc., a call center services provider in Atlanta. She has designed and facilitated hundreds of training programs for management, sales, and customer service departments, including the Call Center Management Institute.

Order Form

QTY.	Item	Member Price	Price	Total
	Call Center Management On Fast Forward: Succeeding In Today's Dynamic Inbound Environment**	**$23.76**	$34.95	
	Call Center Technology Demystified: The No-Nonsense Guide to Bridging Customer Contact Technology, Operations and Strategy**	**$33.96**	$39.95	
	ICMI's Call Center Management Dictionary: The Essential Reference for Contact Center, Help Desk and Customer Care Professionals**	**$21.21**	$24.95	
	ICMI's Pocket Guide to Call Center Management Terms*	**$5.12**	$5.95	
	ICMI Handbook and Study Guide Series Module 1: People Management*** Module 2: Operations Management*** Module 3: Customer Relationship Management*** Module 4: Leadership and Business Management***	**$169.15 ea.**	$199.00 ea.	
	Topical Books: **The Best of *Call Center Management Review*** Call Center Recruiting and New Hire Training* Call Center Forecasting and Scheduling* Call Center Agent Motivation and Compensation* Call Center Agent Retention and Turnover*	**$14.41 ea.**	$16.95 ea.	
	Forms Books Call Center Sample Monitoring Forms** Call Center Sample Customer Satisfaction Forms Book**	**$42.46 ea.**	$49.95 ea.	
	Software QueueView: A Staffing Calculator—CD ROM* Easy Start™ Call Center Scheduler Software—CD-ROM*	**$41.65** **$254.15**	$49.95 $299.00	
	Call Center Humor: The Best of *Call Center Management Review* Volume 3*	**$8.45**	$9.95	
	The Call Centertainment Book*	**$7.61**	$8.95	
	Shipping & Handling @ $5.00 per US shipment, plus .50¢ per* item, $1.00 per** item and $2.00 per*** item. Additional charges apply to shipments outside the US.			
	Tax (5% MD residents, 7% GST Canadian residents)			
	TOTAL (US dollars)			

Please contact us for quantity discounts
For more information on our products, please visit **www.icmi.com**

❑ Please send me a free issue of *Call Center Management Review* (ICMI's journal for members) and information on ICMI's publications, services and membership.

Please ship my order and/or information to:

Name _____

Title _____

Industry _____

Company _____

Address _____

City _____ State _____ Postal Code _____

Telephone ( ) _____

Fax ( ) _____

Email _____

Method of Payment (if applicable)

❑ Check enclosed (Make payable to ICMI Inc.; U.S. Dollars only)

❑ Charge to: ❑ American Express ❑ MasterCard ❑ Visa

Account No. _____

Expiration Date _____

Name on Card _____

Fax order to: 410-267-0962

call us at: 800-672-6177 or 410-267-0700

order online at: www.icmi.com

or mail order to: ICMI Inc.

P.O. Box 6177, Annapolis, MD 21401